C

Cantonese

phrasebook

C000142730

Consultant
Ling Song Chase

First published 2007
Copyright © HarperCollins Publishers
Reprint 10 9 8 7 6 5 4 3 2 1 0
Typeset by Davidson Pre-Press, Glasgow
Printed in Malaysia by Imago

www.collins.co.uk

ISBN 13 978-0-00-724677-9
ISBN 10 0-00-724677-3

Using your phrasebook

Your *Collins Gem phrasebook* is designed to help you locate the exact phrase you need, when you need it, whether on holiday or for business. If you want to adapt the phrases, you can easily see where to substitute your own words using the dictionary section, and the clear, full-colour layout gives you direct access to the different topics.

The Gem phrasebook includes:
- Over 70 topics arranged thematically. Each phrase is accompanied by a simple pronunciation guide which eliminates any problems pronouncing foreign words.

- A top ten tips section to safeguard against any cultural faux pas, giving essential dos and don'ts for situations involving local customs or etiquette.

- Practical hints to make your stay trouble free, showing you where to go and what to do when dealing with everyday matters such as travel or hotels and offering valuable tourist information.

- Face to face sections so that you understand what is being said to you. These example mini-dialogues give you a good idea of what to expect from a real conversation.

- Common announcements and messages you may hear, ensuring that you never miss the important information you need to know when out and about.

- A clearly laid-out dictionary means you will never be stuck for words.

- A basic grammar section which will enable you to build on your phrases.

- A list of public holidays to avoid being caught out by unexpected opening and closing hours, and to make sure you don't miss the celebrations!

It's worth spending time before you embark on your travels just looking through the topics to see what is covered and becoming familiar with what might be said to you.

Whatever the situation, your *Gem phrasebook* is sure to help!

Contents

Pronouncing Cantonese

Although it is not easy for foreigners to pronounce Cantonese, this phrasebook uses standard Latin phonetic sounds to make pronunciation easier.

There are different romanization systems and this book adapts the Yale romanization system to indicate how the characters are pronounced and at what pitch level.

The Yale romanization system was created by Mr Parker Huang and Mr Gerald Kok in the late 1940s and has been widely used by language academics in Cantonese dictionaries and phrasebooks. The Yale romanization system uses consonants and vowels, which look just like English words.

Vowels

Symbol	English equivalent	Cantonese example
a	similar to 'u' in 'bus'	seven 七 chāt
aa	similar to 'ar' in 'far'	duck 鴨 aap
ai	similar to the sound of 'i' in "might"	for 為 waih
au	similar to 'ou' in 'ouch'	have 有 yáuh
e	similar to 'e' in 'let'	thanks 謝 jeh
ei	similar to 'a' in 'lake'	you 你 néih
i	similar to 'ee' in 'bee'	yes 是 sih
iu	similar to 'ui' in 'build'	want 要 yiu
o	similar to the sound of 'o'	good 好 hó
eui	the sound of 'u' in 'Luke' and 'a' in 'lake'	go 去 heui
u	the sound of 'u' in 'Luke' and 'e' in 'let'	live 住 jyuh

Consonants

Symbol	English equivalent	Cantonese example
b,p,m,f d,t,n,l g,k,h	the same sound as in English	
ch	'ch' in 'China'	tea 茶 chàh
ng	'ng' in 'ring'	tooth 牙 ngàh
s	's' in 'sing'	heart 心 sām
w	'w' in 'we'	for 為 waih
y	'y' in 'young'	one 一 yāt

Intonation

According to the Yale system, there are 6 basic tones for pronouncing Cantonese: high flat, high rising, medium flat, low falling, low rising and low flat. In order to make it easier for you to remember them, this book uses the marker above the first vowel in the system to indicate how a character is pronounced. If 'h' is added after the last vowel or at the end of the system it indicates a low pitch level.

Please note, in Yale Cantonese, 'h' is a tonal symbol. Except when it is part of the initial sound, 'h' always denotes a low tone and is not pronounced. It is a tone mark, rather than a sound mark. Thus, '-' above the first vowel of the system indicates a high flat tone. ' ´ ' above the first vowel of system represents the high rising tone. The system without any marker above the first vowel indicates a medium flat tone. ' ` ' above the first vowel, together with 'h' added after the last vowel or at the end of the system shows the low falling tone, ' ´ ' above the fist vowel together with 'h' added just after the last vowel or at the end of the system represents the low rising tone and, lastly, a system without a marker above the first vowel but having 'h' added just after the last vowel or at the end of the system represents the low flat tone.

Examples of these six tones are as follows:

High flat tone:	one 一	yāt
High rising tone:	good/nice 好	hó
Medium flat tone:	go 去	heui
Low falling tone:	ox 牛	ngàuh
Low rising tone:	you 你	néih
Low flat tone:	large 大	daaih

Writing Cantonese

Like in Mandarin Chinese, written Cantonese does not use an alphabet, but instead uses various strokes (such as '⎯', '⏐'). Written Cantonese is made up of 'characters' rather than 'words'.

Grammar

Grammatically, Cantonese is very easy and straight-forward when compared to English and to other European languages:

Verbs do not have different tenses and thus do not change in the past tense or in the past participle. There are no regular and irregular verbs;

The structure of a question is the same as that of a statement – simply adding an extra character 嗎 (mā) to the end of a written sentence turns it into a question;

Chinese words do not have grammatical gender and therefore do not change in the masculine and feminine forms, unlike languages such as French and Italian (although certain Chinese words refer specifically to males or to females, like in English 'pretty' is used for females and 'handsome' for males).

Nouns do not have singular and plural forms.

Top ten tips

•••••••••••••••••••••••••••••••••••••••

1 Chinese people show great respect for the
   wisdom and experience of their elders.
   The senior people present will usually initiate
   the greetings, and you should greet the oldest,
   most senior person before any others.

2 Do not stick your chopsticks into a bowl of rice.
   It reminds the Chinese of the incense sticks they
   burn when they bury their dead.

3 Do not give pears to people in hospital; the word
   for pear is similar to the word for leave (lèih hōi)
   and so insinuates that you want them to die.
   Hong Kong people avoid saying the word 'four'
   or using things in fours as it has a similar sound
   to 'séi' which means death.

4 Business cards should be held in both hands when
   they are being offered or received. When receiving
   another person's card, you should take the time to
   look at it attentively before putting it away.

5 Be aware of the Chinese fear of losing face.
   For example, do not call a restaurant manager
   a 'fuhk mouh yùhn' (waiter/waitress), or
   anything else below their true status.

15

6   It is rude not to accept any consumable item being offered to you (including cigarettes). If you refuse cigarettes you have to come up with a good reason to avoid giving offence!

7   Tipping is left to the customers' discretion. Tipping is expected in most restaurants and hotels. Most restaurants will levy a 10 per cent service charge. However waiters usually expect to be given some loose change. Restaurants that don't add a service charge will expect a 10 per cent tip. Also bellboys, porters, restroom attendants and taxi drivers usually expect some loose change as a tip.

8   Most Chinese women continue using their maiden name even after marriage, but they may indicate their marital status by using 太太 (taai-taai) with their maiden name.

9   In a formal situation you should always exchange business cards and shake hands with the most important person first and then work down, to avoid anyone losing face.

10 Whenever someone pours you tea, use your fingers to knock lightly on the table 3 times to mean 'thank you'. It is polite to wait until everyone's food is served before starting your meal.

Talking to people

Hello/goodbye, yes/no

It is very important to use the appropriate form of greeting in Hong Kong. As with other cultures, the way that you greet somebody will depend on whether you know them or whether they are a stranger.

The most common greeting is 你好 (néih hó).

Please	請 chíng
Thanks (very much)	(多)謝 (dō)-jeh
You're welcome!	不用客氣! ngh-sái haak-hei!

17

| Yes | 是 |
| | sih |

| No | 不是 |
| | bāt-sih |

| Yes, please | 好，謝謝 |
| | hó, jeh-jeh |

| No, thanks | 不用，多謝 |
| | ngh sái, (dō)-jeh |

| OK! | 好！ |
| | hó! |

| Sir/Mr... | ...先生 |
| | ...sīn-sāang |

| Madam/Ms... | ...女仕 |
| | ...núih-sih |

| Mrs... | ...太太 |
| | ...taai-taai |

| Miss... | ...小姐 |
| | ...síu-jé |

Hello	你好 néih-hó	
Hi!	嗨！ hēi!	
Hello! (usually on the phone)	喂！ wai!	
Goodbye	再見 joi-gin	JOY-GEEN
See you later	過一陣見 gwoh-yāt-jahn-gin	
Bye!	再見！ joi-gin!	
See you at seven.	七點見 chāt-dím gin	
See you on Monday!	星期一見！ sīng-kéih-yāt gin!	
Good morning!/ Morning!	早晨！ jó-sàhn!	

Good evening/ Goodnight	晚安 máahn-ōn
See you tomorrow	明天見 mìng-tīn gin
Excuse me!/ Sorry!	對不起! dui-ngh-jyuh!
Excuse me! (to get past in a crowd)	請讓一讓! chíng-yeuhng-yāt-yeuhng!
How are you?	你好嗎? néih-hó-mā?
How have you been?	最近你身體怎麼樣? jui gan néih sān-tái jám mōh yeuhng?
Fine, thanks	好,謝謝 hó, jeh-jeh
Great!	好極了! hó gihk líuh!

| So-so. | 一般 |
| | yāt bāan |

| And you? | 你呢? |
| | néih-nē? |

Long time no see! How are you doing?	好久不見!
	你最近還好嗎?
	hó gáu mó gin! néih jui gan wàanh hó mā?

| I don't understand | 我不明白 |
| | ngóh ngh mìhng-baahk |

| I don't speak Cantonese | 我不識講廣東話 |
| | ngóh ngh-sīk góng gwóng-dūng-wah |

Key phrases

| Do you have a room? | 你們有客房嗎? |
| | néih-mùhn yáuh haak-fòng mā? |

Do you have milk?	你們有牛奶嗎? néih-mùhn yáuh ngàuh-náaih mā?
I'd like...	我想··· ngóh séung...
We'd like...	我們想··· ngóh-mùhn séung...
I'd like an ice cream	我想買一個冰淇淋 ngóh séung máaih yāt-goh bīng-kèih-làhm
Another/ Some more...	另外的/更多的 lihng-ngoih-dīk/ gang-dō-dīk
How much is it?/ How much does it cost?	多少錢? dō-síu-chìhn?
large	大 daaih

small	小 síu
with	加 gā
without	不加 ngh-gā
Where is...?/ Where are...?	···在哪裏? ...joih nàh-léih?
the nearest	離這裏最近的 lèih je-léih jeui-gahn-dīk
How do I get...?	我怎麼···? ngòh jám-mōh...?
to the museum	去博物館 heui bok-maht-góon
to the station	去車站 heui chē-jaahm
to Shanghai	去上海 heui séuhng-hoí

There is.../ There are...	有… yáuh
There isn't.../ There aren't any...	没有… muht yáuh
When?	甚麼時候? sahm-mōh sìh-hauh?
At what time...?	甚麼時間…? sahm-mōh sìh-gāan...?
Today	今天 gām-tīn
tomorrow	明天 mìhng-tīn
Can I...?	我能 … 嗎? ngóh nàhng … mā?
smoke	燒煙 siū-yīn

| taste it | 嘗嘗它 |
| | sèuhng-sèuhng tā |

| How does this work? | 如何使用? |
| | yuèh-hòh sái-yuhng? |

| What does this mean? | 這是甚麼意思? |
| | je-sih sahm-mōh yi-sī? |

Celebrations

| I'd like to wish you... | 我祝願你… |
| | ngóh jūk-yuehn néih… |

| Happy Birthday! | 生日快樂! |
| | sāang-yaht faai-lohk! |

| Happy Anniversary! | 紀念日快樂! |
| | géi-neihm-yaht faai-lohk! |

| Merry Christmas! | 聖誕快樂! |
| | sing-daan faai-lohk! |

| Happy New Year! | 新年快樂! |
| | sān-nìhn faai-lohk! |

| Happy Easter! | 復活節快樂! |
| | fuhk-wuht-jit faai-lohk! |

| Have a good trip! | 一路順風! |
| | yāt-loh suhn-fūng! |

Making friends

Chinese family names are placed first, followed by the given name. For instance, in the name 'Chueng Wai', 'Chueng' is the family name, 'Wai' the given name. Family names usually consist of one syllable, whereas given names can have either one or two syllables.

Chinese people call their close friends and family members by their given names. For example, 'Ma Manlai' may be addressed by close friends as 'Manlai'.

How old are you?	你多大了？ néih dō-daaih-líuh?
I'm ... years old	我 ... 歲了 ngóh ... seui-líuh
Where do you live?	你住在哪裏？ néih jyuh-joih náh-léih?
Where do you (plural) live?	你們住在哪裏？ néih-mùhn jueh-joih náh-léih?
I live in London	我住在倫敦 ngóh jyuh-joih lùhn-dūn
We live in Glasgow	我們住在格拉斯加 ngóh-mùhn jueh-joih gaak-lāai-sī-gā
I'm at school	我在上學 ngóh joih séuhng-hohk
I work	我在工作 ngóh-joih gūng-jok

Talking to people

A 你叫甚麼名字?

néih-giu sahp-mōh mìhng-jih?

What's your name?

B 我叫…

ngóh-giu…

My name is…

A 你是哪裏人?

néih-sih náh-léih-yàhn?

Where are you from?

B 我是英國人，我來自倫敦

ngóh-sih yīng-gwok-yàhn,
 ngóh lòih-jih lùhn-dūn

I am English, from London

A 很高興認識你!

hán-gō-hing yahn-sīk-néih!

Pleased to meet you!

I'm retired	我退休了	ngóh tui-yāu-líuh
I'm...	我…	ngóh...
single	單身	dāan-sān
married	離婚了	git-fān-líuh
divorced	結婚了	lèih-fān-líuh
I have...	我有…	ngóh-yáuh...
a boyfriend	一個男朋友	yāt-goh nàahm-pàhng-yáuh
a girlfriend	一個女朋友	yāt-goh núih-pànhg-yáu
a partner	一位伴侶	yāt-waih buhn-lúih

| I have ... children | 我有 … 孩子 |
| | ngóh-yáuh … hàaih-jí |

| I have no children | 我没有孩子 |
| | ngóh mo hàih-jí |

| Let me introduce you to my friends. | 讓我把你介紹給我的朋友們 |
| | yeuhng ngoh bá néih gaai-siuh kāp ngóh dīk pàhng-yáuh-mùhn |

| I'd like you to meet my husband. | 我想讓你認識一下我的先生 |
| | ngóh séung yeuhng néih yihng-sīk ngóh dīk sīn-sāang |

| Please allow me to introduce these distinguished guests. | 請讓我介紹一下到場的嘉賓 |
| | chíng yeuhng ngóh gaai-siuh yāt-háh dou-chèuhng-dīk gā-bān |

This is Janet.	這是珍妮特
	je sih jān-nèih-dahk
I'm here…	我在這裏…
	ngóh joih je-léih…
on holiday	度假
	doh-gá
on business	公乾
	gūng-gōn
for the weekend	過週末
	gwo-jāu-mooht

Work

In formal situations you should address Chinese people by their family name or full name and the appropriate courtesy title. Unlike English, professional, social and family titles always follow the name.

> **Leisure/interests** (p 98) > **Sport** (p 106)   31

Mr Lau	劉先生	làuh sīn-sāang
Mr Li Nam	李楠先生	léih nàamh sin-sāang
Mrs Lau	劉太太	làuh taai-taai
Miss Lau	劉小姐	làuh síu-jé
Ms Lau	劉女仕	làuh núih-sih
Dr Ma	馬醫生	máh yī-sāang
Prof Wong	徐教授	wòhng gaau-sauh

What do you do?	你是做哪一行業的?	néih sih jouh náh yāt hòhng-yihp dīk?
Do you like your job?	你喜歡你的工作嗎?	néih-héi-fōon néih-dīk gūng-jok mā?
I'm ... a doctor	我是 … 一名醫生	ngóh-sih … yāt-mìhng-yī-sāang
a manager	一名經理	yāt-mìhng gīng-léi

32

| a housewife | 一名家庭主婦 |
| | yāt-mìhng gā-tìhng-júe-fóoh |

| I work from home | 我在家裏工作 |
| | ngóh joih gā-léih gūng-jok |

| I'm self-employed | 我是自謀職業者 |
| | ngáh sih jih-màuh-jīk-yīp-jé |

Weather

| weather forecast | 天氣預報 |
| | tīn-hei yueh-bo |

| changeable weather | 多變的氣候 |
| | dōh-bin-dīk hei-hauh |

| fine | 好 |
| | hó |

| bad | 壞 |
| | waaih |

| cloudy | 多云 |
| | dōh-wàhn |

It's sunny	天晴 tīn–chìhng
It's raining	落雨 lohk–yuéh
It's snowing	落雪 lohk–suet
It's windy	刮風 gwaat–fūng
What a lovely day!	天氣真好！ tīn–hei jān–hóu!
What awful weather!	天氣真差！ tīn–hei jān–chā!
What will the weather be like tomorrow?	明天天氣會怎麼樣呢? mìhng–tīn tīn–hei wúih jám–mōh–yeuhng nē?
Do you think it's going to rain?	你認為天會落雨嗎? néih jihng–wàih tīn wúih lohk–yuéh mā?

It's very hot/cold/ today	今天很熱/冷 gām-tīn hán-yiht/láahng
Do you think there will be a storm?	你認為會刮風暴嗎? néih jihng-wàih wúihh gwaat-fūng-boh mā?
Do you think it will snow?	你認為會落雪嗎? néih jihng-wàih wúih luoh-suet mā?
Will it be foggy?	會有霧嗎? wúih yáuh-moh mā?
What is the temperature?	氣溫是多少? hei-wān sih dōh-síu?

Weather

Getting around

Asking the way

If you want to attract the attention of someone you do not know – for example, in the street – you say 請問 (chíng mahn).

對面的	dui-mihn dīk	opposite
旁邊的 póhng-bīn-dīk		next to
鄰近	lùhn-gahn	near to
紅綠燈 hùhng-luhk-dāng		traffic lights
十字路口 sahp-jih-loh-háu		crossroads
(路)邊	(loh)-bīn	corner (of road)

36

A 請問，我怎麼去車站?

chíng-mahn, ngóh jám-mōh heui chē-jaahm?

Excuse me, how do I get to the station?

B 一直往前走，過了教堂就轉左/右

yāt jihk wóhng chìhn jáu, gwo-líuh gaau-tòhng jauh jyun jó/yauh

Keep straight on, after the church turn left/right

A 遠嗎?

yúehn mā?

Is it far?

B 唔遠，200米/5分鐘

ngh-yúehn, yih-baak-máih/ngh-fān-jūng

No, 200 metres/five minutes

A 謝謝你!

jeh-jeh-néih!

Thank you!

B 不用客氣

ngh-sái-haak-hei

You're welcome

Asking the way

37

| We're lost | 我們迷路了 |
| | ngóh-mùhn mài-loh-líuh |

| We're looking for... | 我們正在找… |
| | ngóh-mùhn jing-joih jáau... |

| Is this the right way to...? | 這是去 … 的路嗎? |
| | je-sih heui … dīk-loh mā? |

Can I/we walk there?	我/
	我們可以步行去那裏嗎?
	ngóh/ngóh-mùhn hó-yi
	boh-hing-heui náh-léih mā?

How do I/ we get onto the motorway?	我/我們怎麼上高速公路?
	ngóh/ngóh-mùhn jám-mōh
	séuhng gō-chūk-gūng loh?

| to the museum? | 去博物館? |
| | heui bok-maht-góon? |

| to the shops? | 去商店? |
| | heui sēung-dim? |

| Can you show me on the map? | 你能在地圖上指給我看嗎？ |
| | néih-nàhng joih deih-tòh-séuhng jí-kāp-ngóh-tái mā? |

YOU MAY HEAR...

在那裏 joih náh-léih	down there
在後面 joih-hauh-mihn	behind
然後再問人 yìhn-hauh joi-mahn-yàhn	then ask again

Asking the way

> **Maps and guides** (p 91)

Bus and coach

FACE TO FACE

A 請問，哪輛公共汽車去市/鎮中心?

chíng-mahn, náh-léung gūng-guhng-hei-chē heui-sìh/jan-júng-sām?

Excuse me, which bus goes to the city/town centre?

B 15路汽車

sahp-ngh-loh-hei-chē

Number 15

A 公共汽車在哪裏?

gūng-guhng-hei-chē joih-náh-léih?

Where is the bus stop?

B 那裏，在右邊

náh-léih, joih-yauh bīn

There, on the right

A 我在哪裏可以買車票?

ngóh joih-náh-léi hó-yíh máaih chē-piu?

Where can I buy the tickets?

B 在售票處

joih sauh-piu-chyu

At the ticket office

Is there a bus/ tram to...?	有公共汽車/電車去…?
	yáuh-gūng-guhng-hei-chē/ dihn-chē heui...?

Where do I catch the bus/tram to...?	我在哪裏搭去 … 的公共汽車/電車?
	ngóh joih náh-léih dāap heui … dīk gūng-guhng-hei-chē/ dihn-chē?

We're going to...	我們正在去…
	ngóh-mùhn jing-joih-heui...

How much is it to go...?	去 … 要多少錢?
	heui … yiu dōh-síu-chìhn?

to the city/ town centre	去市/鎮中心
	heui-síh/jan-jūng-sām

to the beach	去海灘
	heui-hói-tāan

How often are the buses to...?	每隔多長時間就有一班公共汽車去…?
	múih-gaak dōh-chèuhng-sìh-gāan jauh-yáuh yāt-bāan gūng-guhng-hei-chē heui...?

When is the first/the last bus to...?	去…的第一班/最後一班公共汽車是甚麼時間?
	heui...dīk daih-yāt-bāan/jeui-hauh-yāt-bāan gūng-guhng-hei-chē sìh-sahm-mōh-sìh-gaan?

Please tell me when to get off	到時候請你告訴我落車
	do-sìh-hauh chíng-néih go-sou ngóh lohk-chē

Please let me off	請讓我落車
	chíng yeuhng-ngóh lohk-chē

This is my stop	我要在這一站落車
	ngóh yiu-joih je-yāt-jaahm lohk-chē

42

你在這一站落車 néih joih je-yāt-jaahm- lohk-chē	This is your stop
請搭地鐵， 　搭地鐵會快些 chíng daap deih-tit, daap deih-tit wúih faai sē	Take the metro, it's quicker

Bus and coach

Metro

....

入口	yahp-háu	entrance
出口	chūt-háu	way out/exit
每周/每月 múih-jāu/múih-yueht		weekly/monthly

A 24-hour/ 48-hour ticket	一張24/48個小時以內可以使用的車票 yāt-jēung yih-sahp-sèi/sei-sahp-baat goh-síu-sìh yíh-noih hó-yíh sái-yuhng-dīk chē-piu
Where is the nearest metro?	離這裏最近的地鐵站在哪裏? lèih je-léuih jeui-gahn-dīk deih-tit-jaahm joih náh-léuih?
How does the ticket machine work?	如何使用售票機? yùeh-hòh sái-yuhng sauh-piu-gēi?

44

| I'm going to... | 我正在去··· |
| | ngóh jing-joih heui... |

| Do you have a map of the metro? | 你有一張地鐵圖嗎? |
| | néih yáuh yāt-jēung deih-tit-tòuh mā? |

| How do I get to...? | 我怎麼去···? |
| | ngóh jám-mōh heui...? |

| Do I have to change? | 我要換車嗎? |
| | ngóh yiu wuhn-chē mā? |

| What is the next stop? | 下一站是哪一站? |
| | hah-yāt-jaahm sih náh-yāt-jaahm? |

| Excuse me! | 請讓一讓! |
| | Chíng yeuhng-yāt-yeuhng! |

| This is my stop | 我要在這一站落車 |
| | ngóh yiu joih-je-yāt-jaahm lohk-chē |

| Please let me out | 請讓我出去 |
| | chíng yeuhng-ngóh chūt-heui |

Train

站檯 jaahm-tòih	platform
售票處 sauh-piu-chyu	ticket office
時刻表 sìh-hāk-bīu	timetable
誤點 ngh-dím	delay (appears on train noticeboards)
行李寄存 hàhng-léih gei-chyùhn	left luggage

FACE TO FACE

A 下一趟去 … 的火車是甚麼時間?
hah-yāt-tong heui … dīk fóh-chē sih sahm-mō sìh-gāan?
When is the next train to....?

B 下午五點十分
hah-ngh ngh-dím-sahp-fān
At 17.10

A 我想買三張票
ngóh-séung máaih sāam-jēung-piu
I'd like 3 tickets, please

B 單程還是雙程?
dāan-chìhng-wàahn-sih sēung-chìhng?
Single or return?

Where is the station?	車站在哪裏? chē-jaahm joih náh-léih?
1 ticket/2 tickets to...	一/兩張去 ⋯ 的票 yāt/léuhng-jēung heui ⋯ dīk-piu
first/second class	頭等/二等 tàuh-dáng/yih-dáng
smoking/ non smoking	吸煙/禁煙區 kāp-yīn/gām-yīn-kēui
Is there a supplement to pay?	要付附加費嗎? yiu fuh fuh-gā-fai mā?

Train

| Do I have to change? | 我要換車嗎? |
| | ngóh-yiu wuhn-chē mā? |

| Which platform does it leave from? | 從哪個站檯出發? |
| | chùhng náh-goh jaahm-tòih chūt-faat? |

| Is this the train for...? | 這是去 … 的火車嗎? |
| | je-sih heui … dīk-fó-chē mā? |

| Does it stop at...? | 它在 … 停嗎? |
| | tā-joih … tìhng mā? |

| When does it arrive in...? | 它甚麼時候到達…? |
| | tā sahm-mō sìh-hauh do-daaht...? |

| Please tell me when we get to... | 到達 … 時請告訴我 |
| | do-daaht … sìh chíng-gou-sou ngóh |

| Is there a restaurant car? | 有餐車嗎? |
| | yáuh chāan-chē mā? |

Is this seat free?	有人坐這個座位嗎?
	yáuh yàhn-chóh je-go joh-waih mā?

Excuse me! (to get past)	請讓一讓!
	chíng-yeuhng-yāt-yeuhng!

Taxi

I want a taxi	我想叫一輛出租車
	ngóh séung-giu yāt-léung chēut-jō-chē

Where can I get a taxi?	我在哪裏可以叫一輛出租車?
	ngóh joih náh-léih hó-yíh giu yā t-leuhng chēut-jō-chē?

Please order me a taxi now	請現在為我叫一輛出租車
	chíng yihn-joih waih ngóh giu yāt-léung chēut-jōu-chē

> **Luggage** (p 127)

Please order me a taxi for...	請在···點為我叫一輛出租車 chíng joih...dím waih ngoh giu yāt-léung chēut-jōu-che
How much will it cost to go to...?	去 ··· 要多少錢? heui ... yiu dō-síu-chìhn?
to the station	去車站 heui chē-jaahm
to the airport	去機場 heui gēi-chèuhng
to this address	去這個地址 heui je-go deih ji
How much is it?	多少錢? dō-síu-chìhn?
Why is it so much?	為甚麼這麼多錢? waih-sahm-mō je-mō-dō-chìhn?

It's more than on the meter	收費多於計費表上顯示的價錢 sāu-fai dō-yū gai-fai-bīu-seuhng hín-sih-dīk ga-chìhn
Keep the change	不用找零錢給我 ngh-sái jáau lìhng-chìhn kāp-ngóh
Sorry, I don't have any change	對不起，我没有零錢 dui-ngh-jyuh, ngóh-mòh lìhng-chìn
I'm in a hurry	我要趕時間 ngóh-yiu gón-sìh-gāan
Can you go a little faster?	你可以開快一些嗎? néih ho-yíh hōi-faai-yāt-sē mā?
I have to catch...	我要趕… ngóh-yiu-gón…
a train	一趟火車 yāt-tong fó-chē

| a plane | 一架飛機 |
| | yāt-ga fēi-gēi |

Boat and ferry

....

| Have you a timetable? | 你有一張時刻表嗎? |
| | néih-yáuh yāt-jēung-sìh-hāk-bīu mā? |

| Is there a car ferry to...? | 有去 … 的載車渡輪嗎? |
| | yáuh heui…dīk joi-chē-douh-lèuhn mā? |

| How much is a ticket...? | 一張去 … 的票要多少錢? |
| | yāt-jēung heui … dīk-piu yiu dō-síu-chìhn? |

| single/return | 單程/雙程 |
| | dāan-chìhng/sēung-chìhng |

| How much is it for a car and ... people? | 一輛車和 … 人要多少錢? |
| | yāt-léung chē wòh … yàhn yiu-dō-síu-chìhn? |

> **Luggage** (p 127)

| When is the first/ the last boat? | 第一班/最後一班輪船是甚麼時間的?
daih-yāt-bāan/jeui-hauh
yāt-bāan lùhn-sùehn sih
sahm-mō sìh-gāan-dīk? |

YOU MAY HEAR...

| 這是最後一班輪船
je-sih jeui-hauh yāt-
bāan lùhn-sùehn | This is the last boat |

Air travel

抵達	dái-daaht	arrivals
起飛	héi-fēi	departures
國際的	gwok-jàih-dīk	international
國内的	gwok-noih-dīk	domestic
登機口	dāng-gēi-háu	boarding gate

How do I get to the airport?	我怎麼去機場? ngóh jám-mō heui gēi-chèuhng?
Is there a bus to the airport?	有公共汽車去機場嗎? yáuh gūng-guhng-hei-chē heui gēi-chèuhng mā?
Where is the luggage for the flight from...?	來自 ⋯ 航班的行李在哪裏? lòih-jih ... hòhng-bāan-dīk hàhng-lèih-joih-náh-léih?
Where can I change some money?	我在哪裏可以換錢? ngóh-joih náh-léih hó-yíh wuhn-chìhn?
How much is it to go to ... by taxi?	乘搭出租車去 ⋯ 要多少錢? sìhng-dāap chēut-jō-chē heui...yiu dō-síu-chìhn?

YOU MAY HEAR...

請在 ⋯ 號登機口 登機 chíng joih ⋯ hoh dāng-gēi-háu dāng-gēi	Boarding will take place at gate number...
請迅速去 ⋯ 號登 機口 chíng sun-chūk heui ⋯ hoh dāng-gēi-háu	Go immediately to gate number...

Customs control

• •

護照	wooh-jiu	passport/s
海關	hói-gw	customs

Do I have to pay duty on this?	我要支付该商品的關稅嗎? ngóh-yiu jī-fuh gōi-sēung-bán-dīk gwāan-sui mā?

55

It's for my own personal use/ for a present

這是我自用的/送人的 禮品

je-sih ngóh jih-yuhng-dīk/ sung-yàhn-dīk láih-bán

We are on our way to... (if in transit through a country)

我們正在轉機去…

ngóh-mùhn jing-joih juen-gēi-heui...

The child/children is/are on this passport

孩子/們的名字在這本護 照上

hàaih-jí/ mùhn dīk mìhng-jih joih jéh bún wuh-jiu seuhng

Driving

Car hire

駕駛执照 ga-sái-jáp-jiu	driving licence
全保險 chùehn-bó-hím	fully comprehensive insurance

I want to hire a car for ... days

我想租一輛車 ⋯ 天
ngóh séung jō-yāt-léung-chē
... tīn

with automatic gears

自動檔
jih-duhng-dóng

What are your rates...?

你們的收費是多少⋯?
néih-mùhn-dīk sāu-fáih sih
dō-síu...?

per day	每天 múih-tīn
per week	每週 múih-jāu
How much is the deposit?	定金是多少? dihng-gām sih-dō-síu?
Do you take credit cards?	你們接受信用卡嗎? néig-mùhn jip-sauh sun-yuhng-kā mā?
Is there a mileage (kilometre) charge?	有按公里數的收費嗎? yáuh on-gūng-léih-so-dīk sāu-fáih mā?
How much is it?	多少錢? dō-síu-chìhn?
Does the price include fully comprehensive insurance?	收費包括全保險嗎? sāu-fáih bāau-koot chùehn-bó-hím mā?

Must I return the car here?	我必須在這裏還車嗎? ngóh bīt-sūi joih-je-léih wàahn-chē mā?
By what time?	在甚麼時間以前? joih sahm-mō sìh-gāan yíh-chìhn?
I'd like to leave it in...	我想把它留在… ngóh séung bá tā làuh joih…

YOU MAY HEAR...

還車時油箱必須是加滿的 wàahn-chē-sìh yàuh-seung bīt-sūi-sih gā-móohn-dīk	Please return the car with a full tank

Driving and petrol

The speed limits in Hong Kong are 50 km/h on ordinary roads and 70-110 km/h on express roads.

| Can I/we park here? | 我/我們可以在這裏停放車嗎? |
| | ngóh/ngóh-mùhn hó-yíh joih je-léih tìhng-fong-chē mā? |

How long for?

可以停放多長時間?
hó-yíh tìhng-fong dō-chèuhng-sìh-gāan?

Which junction is it for...?

去 … 是哪一個出口?
heui … sih náh-yāt-go chūt-háu?

Do I/we need snow chains?

我/我們需要雪链嗎?
ngóh/ngóh-mùhn sūi-yiu suet-lihn mā?

Fill it up, please

請加满油
chíng gā-móohn yàuh

Driving

4星	sei-sīng	4 star
柴油	cháai-yáu	diesel
無鉛汽油 mòh-yùehn-hei-yàu		unleaded

Please check the oil/the water	請检查機油/水 chíng gím-chàh gēi-yàuh/séui	
...100 yuan worth of unleaded petrol	•••100圓的無鉛汽油 ...yāt-bai-yùehn-dīk mòh-yùehn-hei-yàu	
Where is...?	•••在哪裏? ...joih-náh-léih?	
the air line/water	充氣管/水 chūng-hei-góon/séui	
Pump number...	•••號泵 ...hoh-bām	
Where do I pay?	我在哪裏付款? ngóh-joih náh-léih fuh-fóon?	

| Can I pay by credit card? | 我可以使用信用卡付款嗎? |
| | ngóh hó-yíh sái-yuhng sun-yuhng-kā fuh-fún mā? |

YOU MAY HEAR...

| 你需要一些機油/一些水
néih sūi-yiu yāt-sē gēi-yàuh/yāt-sē séui | You need some oil/some water |
| 一切都好
yāt-chai-dō-hó | Everything is OK |

Breakdown

A garage that does repairs is known as a 修車行 (sāu-chē-hòhng).

| Can you help me? | 你能幫助我嗎?
néih nànhg bōng-joh ngóh mā? |

My car has broken down	我的車出了故障 ngóh-dīk chē chūt-líuh goo-jeung
I've run out of petrol	我没汽油了 ngóh mo hei-yàuh-líuh
Can you tow me to the nearest garage?	你能把我的車拖到最近的修車行嗎? néih nàhng bá ngóh-dīk chē tō-do jeui-gahn-dīk sāu-chē-hòhng mā?
Do you have parts for a (make of car)...?	你有 ⋯ 車的零件嗎? néih-yáuh … chē-dīk lìhng-gihn mā?
There's something wrong with the...	⋯壞了 …waaih-líuh
Can you replace...?	你能更換 ⋯ 嗎? néih-nàhng gang-wuhn … mā?

Car parts

. . . .

The ... doesn't work/The ... don't work	…不運作	…ngh-wahn-jok
accelerator	加速器	gā-chūk-hei
alternator	交流發電機	gāau-làuh-faat-dihn-gēi
battery	電池	dihn-chìh
bonnet	發動機罩蓋	faat-duhng-gēi-jaau-gaai
brakes	刹車閘	saat-chē-jaahp
choke	阻風門	jó-fūng-muhn
clutch	離合器	lèih-hahp-hei
distributor	分销商	fān-sīu-sēung
engine	發動機	faat-duhng-gēi
exhaust	廢氣	fai-hei
fuse	保險絲	bó-hím-sī

gears	換檔	wuhn-dong
handbrake	手刹	sáu-saat
headlights	車頭燈	chē-tàu-dāng
ignition	點火	dím-fó
indicator	顯示器	hín-sih-hei
radiator	散熱器	sáan-yiht-hei
reverse gear	後換檔	hauh-wuhn-dong
seat belt	安全帶	ōn-chùehn-daai
spark plug	火花塞	fó-fā-sāk
steering	轉向	júen-heung
steering wheel	方向盤	fōng-heung-pòohn
tyre	輪胎	lùhn-tōi
wheel	車輪	chē-lùhn
windscreen	擋風玻璃	dóng-fūng-bōh-lèih

windscreen washer	擋風玻璃 清洗器	dóng-fūng-bōh-lèih chīng-sái-hei
windscreen wiper	擋風玻璃 刮水器	dóng-fūng-bōh-lèih gwaat-súi-hei

Driving

Staying somewhere

Hotel (booking)

single room
單人房
dāan-yàhn-fòhng

double room
雙人房
sēung-yàhn-fòhng

private facilities
私人設施
sī-yàhn chit-sī

number of adults
多少大人
dō-síu daaih-yàhn

number of
  children
多少小孩
dōh-síu síu-hàaih

A 我想預定一間單人房/雙人房

ngóh-séung yueh-dihng yāt-gāan dāan-yàhn-
    fòhng/sēung-yàhn-fòhng

I'd like to book a single/double room

B 幾個晚上?

gēi-go máahn-séuhng?

For how many nights?

A 一/…個晚上

yāt/…go máahn-séuhng

for one night/… nights from… till…

How much is it per night/ per week?	每晚/週多少錢? múih-máahn/jāu dō-síu chìhn?
Do you have a room for tonight?	你們這裏今晚還有一間客房嗎? néih-mùhn je-léih gām-máahn wàahn-yáuh yāt-gāan haak-fòhng mā?

Staying somewhere

with bath	有浴缸 yáuh-yueh-gōng
with shower	有淋浴 yáuh-làhm-yueh
a double bed	雙人床 sēung-yàhn-chòhng
with twin-beds	兩張單人床 léuhng-jēung-dāan-yàhn- chòhng
with an extra bed for a child	額外的一張小孩床 ngaahk-ngoih-dīk yāt-jēung síu-hàaih-chòhng
Is breakfast included?	早餐包括在內嗎? jó-chāan bāau-koot joih- noih mā?
Have you got anything cheaper?	你們有其它便宜一些的 房間嗎? néih-mùhn yáuh kèih-tā pìhn-yìh-yāt-sē-dīk fòhng-gāan mā?

I'd like to see the room	我想看看房間 ngóh séung tái-tái fòhng-gāan

YOU MAY HEAR...

我們這裏已經住滿了客人 ngóh-mùhn je-léih yíh-gīng jyuh-móohn-líuh haak-yàhn	We're full
請問你叫甚麼名字? chíng-mahn néih giu sahm-mō mìhng-jih?	Your name, please
請用電郵或傳真確認 chíng-yuhng dihn-yāu aahk chùehn-jān ok-yahn	Please confirm ... by e-mail/by fax

Hotel (desk)

●●●

Many hotels are now signposted in towns. The
Chinese word for a hotel is 旅館 (lúih-góon)

| I booked a room... | 我已經用叫… |
| | ngóh yíh-gīng yuhng giu... |

in the name of...	的名字定了一間客房
	dīk-mìhng-jih dihng-líuh
	yāt-gāan haak-fòhng

Where can I park the car?	我可以在哪裏停放車?
	ngóh hó-yíh joih náh-léih
	tìhng-fong chē?

What time is ... dinner/ breakfast?	幾點 … 吃晚飯/早餐?
	géi-dím...sihk-máahn-faahn/
	jó-chāan?

| The key, please | 請把鎖匙給我 |
| | chíng bá só-sìh kāp ngóh |

The room number is...	房間號碼是… fòhng-gāan hoh-máh sih…
Are there any messages for me?	我有留言嗎? ngóh yáuh làuh-yìhn mā?
Can I send a fax?	我能發送一份傳真嗎? ngóh-nàhng faat-sung yāt-fahn chùehn-jān mā?
I'm leaving tomorrow	我明天離開 ngóh mìhng-tīn lèih-hōi
Please prepare the bill	請準備帳單 chíng jún-beih jeung-dāan

Camping

●●●●●●●●●●●●●●●●●●●●●●●●●●●●●●●●●●●

垃圾	laahp-saap	rubbish
飲用水	yám-yuhng-súi	drinking water
電源	dihn-yùehn	electric point

Is there a restaurant/ a self-service café on the campsite?

在野營地有餐館/
自助餐廳嗎？

joih yéh-yìhng-deih yáuh chāan-góon/jih-joh-chāan-tēng mā?

Do you have any vacancies?

你們這裏還有客房嗎？

néih-mùhn je-léih wàahn-yáuh haak-fòhng mā?

How much is it per night?

每晚多少錢？

múih-máahn dō-síu chìhn?

per tent

每個帳篷

múih-go jeung-pùhng

| per caravan | 每輛拖車 |
| | múih-léung tō-chē |

| per person | 每人 |
| | múih-yàhn |

| Does the price include...? showers/ hot water/ electricity | 價錢包括 ⋯ 嗎? 淋浴/熱水/電 |
| | ga-chìhn bāau-koot ... mā? làhm-yueh/yiht-súi/ dihn |

| We'd like to stay for ... nights | 我們想住 ⋯ 個晚上 |
| | ngóh-mùhn séung-jyuh ... go máahn-séuhng |

Self-catering

Who do we contact if there are problems?
如果有問題我們聯絡誰?
yùeh-gwó yáuh mahn-tàih
ngóh-mùhn lùehn-lok
bīn-go-yàhn?

How does the heating work?
暖氣如何工作?
núehn-hei yùeh-hòh
gūng-jok?

Is there always hot water?
所有時間都有熱水嗎?
só yáuh sìh-gāan dō-yáuh
yiht-súi mā?

Where is the nearest supermarket?
離這裏最近的超市在哪裏?
lèih je-léih jeui-gahn-dīk
chīu-síh joih náh-léih?

Where do we leave the rubbish?
我們把垃圾放在哪裏?
ngóh-mùhn bá laahp-saap
fong-joih náh-léih?

> **Sightseeing and tourist office** (p 96)

Self-catering

75

Shopping

Shopping phrases

Opening hours are approximately 8.30 am to 10 pm Monday to Sunday. Opening hours tend to be longer in the summer. Some supermarkets are open all day.

FACE TO FACE

A 你想買甚麼?

néih séuhng-máaih sahm-mō?

What would you like?

B 你們有 … 嗎?

néih-mùhn yáuh … mā?

Do you have...?

A 有，給你。你還要其他它東西嗎?

yáuh, kāp-néih. néih wàahn-yiu kèih-tā dūng-sāi mā?

Certainly, here you are. Anything else?

Where is...?	…在哪裏? …joih-náh-léih?
I'm just looking	我先看看 ngóh sīn-tái-hah
I'm looking for a present for...	我想買個禮物給我的… ngóh séung máaih goh láih-maht kāp ngóh-dīk…
my mother	媽媽 mā-mā
a child	孩子 hàaih-jí
Where can I buy...?	我在哪裏可以買…? ngóh joih náh-léih hó-yíh máaih…?
shoes	鞋 hàaih
gifts	禮物 láih-maht

| It's too expensive for me | 這太貴了 je taai-gwai líuh |
| Can you give me a discount? | 你可以給我打折嗎? néih hó-yíh kāp-ngóh dá-jit mā? |

Shops

•••••••••••••••••••••••••••••••••

廉售	lìhm-sauh	sale
打折	dá-jit	discount

baker's	麵包店	mihn-bāau-dim
butcher's	肉店	yuhk-dim
cake shop	蛋糕店	daahn-gō-dim
clothes	衣物店	yī-maht-dim
fruit shop	水果店	séui-gwó-dim
gifts	禮品店	láih-bán-dim
grocer's	雜貨店	jaahp-fo-dim
hairdresser's	髮廊	faat-lòhng

newsagent	報攤	bo-tāan
optician	眼鏡商	ngáahn-geng-sēung
perfume shop	香水店	hēung-séui-dim
pharmacy	藥店	yeuhk-dim
photographic shop	相館	seung-góon
shoe shop	鞋店	hàaih-dim
sports shop	運動品商店	wahn-duhng-bán-sēung-dim
supermarket	超市	chīu-síh
tobacconist's	香煙店	hēung-yīn-dim
toys	玩具	wuhn-geuih

Supermarket

I would like to buy...	我想買…	ngóhh-séung-máaih…
biscuits	餅乾	béng-gōn

bowl	碗	wóon
bread	麵包	mihn-bāau
butter	牛油	ngàuh-yàuh
cheese	奶酪	náaih-lok
chicken	雞	gāi
chocolate	巧克力	háau-hāk-lihk
chopsticks	筷子	faai-jí
coffee (instant)	速溶咖啡	chūk-yùhng-ga-fē
cooking oil	油	yàuh
cream	奶油	náaih-yàuh
crisps	薯片	syùh-pin
eggs	蛋	dáan
fish	魚	yùeh
flour	麵粉	mihn-fán
jam	果醬	gwóh-jeung
juice, orange	果汁、橙汁	gwó-jāp, cháang-jāp
milk	鮮奶	sín-náaih

oat	麥片	màkh-pin
olive oil	橄欖油	gám-láahm-yàuh
pepper	胡椒	wòoh-jīu
plate	碟子	dihp-jí
rice	大米	daaih-máih
rolling-pin	擀麵棍	gám-mihn-gwan
salt	鹽	yìmh
soya sauce	生抽	sāang-chāu
spatula	鍋鏟	wōh-cháan
spoon	匙羹	chìh-gāng
sugar	糖	tòhng
tea	茶	chàh
tomatoes (tin)	番茄罐頭	fāan-kèh-goon-tàuh
vinegar	醋	cho
whisk	攪拌器	gáau-poon-hei
wok	炒菜鍋	cháau-choi-wōh
yoghurt	酸奶	sūen-náaih

Food (fruit and veg)

Fruit 水果

apples	蘋果	pìhng-gwó
apricots	杏子	hahng-jí
bananas	香蕉	hēung-jīu
cherries	櫻桃	yīng-tòh
grapefruit	葡萄柚	pòh-tòh-yáu
grapes	葡萄	pò-tòh
lemon	檸檬	nìhng-mūng
melon	瓜	gwā
oranges	橙子	cháang-jí
peaches	桃子	tòh-jí
pears	雪梨	suet-lèih
plums	梨子	léih-jí
strawberries	草莓	chó-mèih
watermelon	西瓜	sāi-gwā

Vegetables 蔬菜

asparagus	芦笋	lòuh-séun
aubergine	茄子	kèh-jí
carrots	紅蘿蔔	hùhng lòh-baahk
cauliflower	菜花	choi-fā
celery	芹菜	kàhn-choi
cucumber	黄瓜	wòhng-gwā
garlic	大蒜	daaih-suen
mushrooms	蘑菇	mòh-gū
onions	洋葱	yèuhng-chūng
peas	豌豆	wūn-dauh
pepper	青椒	chēng-jīu
potatoes	土豆	to-dauh
salad	涼拌生菜	lèuhng-buhn-sāang-choi
spinach	菠菜	bō-choi
tomatoes	番茄	fāan-kèh

Food (fruit and veg)

> **Measurements and quantities** (p 152)

Clothes

．．．．．．．．．．．．．．．．．．．．．．．．．．．．．．

FACE TO FACE

A 我可以試穿嗎?
ngóh hó-yíh sìh-chūen mā?
May I try this on?

B 請往這邊走
chíng wóhng je-bīn jáu
Please come this way

A 你們有小/中/大碼嗎?
néih-mùhn yáuh síu/jūng/daaih-máh mā?
Do you have a small/medium/large size?

B 你穿多大尺寸的衣服?
néih chūen dō-daaih chek-chuen-dīk yī-fuhk?
What size (clothes) do you take?

bigger	大些	daaih-sē
smaller	小些	síu-sē

in other colours　　其它颜色
　　　　　　　　kèih-tā ngàahn-sīk

YOU MAY HEAR...

| 你穿多大尺碼的鞋?
néih-chūen dō-daaih
chek-máh-dīk hàaih? | What shoe size do
you take? |
| 這种颜色我們只有
這一尺寸
je-jūng ngáan-sīk ngóh-
mùhn jí-yáuh je-yāt
chek-chuen | In this colour we only
have this size |

Department store

I would like
to buy ... for my
wife/girlfriend/
husband/
boyfriend.

我想為我的太太/
女朋友/先生/
男朋友買···

ngóhh séung waih ngóhh-
dīk-tàih-tai/núih- pàhng-
yáuh/sīn-sāang/náam-
pàhng-yáuh máaih...

blouse	女上衣	núih-séungh-yī
briefcase	公文包	gūng-mành-bāau
coat	大衣	daaih-yī
dress	連衣裙	lìhn-yī-kwàhn
handbag	手袋	shao-daai
jacket	外套	ngoih-to
jumper	毛衣	làahm-sāam
knickers	女内褲	núih-dái-fu
pyjamas	睡衣	sui-yī
shirt	襯衫	chan-sāam
shoes	鞋子	hàaih-jí
shorts	短褲	dúen-fu
silk dress	真絲連衣裙	jān-sī-lình-yī-kwàhn
silk scarf	絲巾	sī-gān
silk tie	真絲領帶	jān-sī-língh-daai
skirt	短裙	dúen-kwàhn
socks	短襪	dúen-maht

suitcase	手提箱	shao-tàih-sēung
suits	西裝	sāi-jōng
swimsuit	游泳衣	yau-wihng-yī
t-shirt	T恤衫	T-sūt-sāam
tights	褲襪	foo-maht
trainers	運動鞋	wahn-duhng-hàaih
trousers	長褲	chèuhng-fu
underpants	内衣褲	dái-sāam-foo

Bookshop/music shop

字典	jih-dín	dictionary
小說	síu-suet	novel
唐詩	tòhng-sī	Tang poetry
光碟	gwōng-dihp	CD
歌曲	gō-kūk	songs

Do you have an English-Chinese dictionary?	你們有中英文字典嗎? néih-mùhn yáuh jūng-yīng-mành jih-dín mā?
I would like to buy an English novel.	我想買一本英文小說 ngóhh-séung máaih-yāt-bóon yīng-mành síu-suet
Do you have collected poems of Tang poetry?	你們有唐詩集嗎? néih-mùhn yáuh tòngh-sī-jaahp mā?
How much does one CD cost?	一盒光碟要多少錢? yāt-hahp gwōng-dihp yiu dōh-síu-chình?
I would like to buy some CDs of Chinese songs.	我想買一些中國歌曲的光碟 ngóhh-séung-máaih yāt-sē jūng-gwok-gōh-kūk-dīk gwōng-dihp
Do you have any English news-papers/books?	你們有英文報紙/書嗎? néih-mùhn yáuh yīng-mành bo-jí/syū mā?

> **Paying** (p 125)

Antique shop

景泰藍 gíng-taai-làamh	Cloisonné
明瓷器 mìngh-chìh-hei	Ming porcelain
玉石 yueh-sehk	jade
兵馬俑 bīng-mā-yúng	terracotta
書法 sūe-faat	calligraphy
鴉片煙斗 ā-pin-yīn-dáu	opium pipe

Do you have any Chinese Cloisonné?　你們有中國景泰藍嗎?
néih-mùhn yáuh jūng-gwok gíng-taai-làamh mā?

Is this Ming porcelain?　這是明瓷器嗎?
je-sih mìngh-chìh-hei mā?

> **Paying** (p 125)

I would like to buy a jade bracelet

我想買一隻玉石手鐲

ngóhh séung máaih yāt-jek yueh-sehk-shao-juhk

Do you have the original terracotta?

你們有原製的兵馬俑嗎?

néih-mùhn yáuh yùenh-jai-dīk bīng-mā-yúng mā?

I am interested in buying a mounted picture of Chinese calligraphy

我想買一幅裱好的中國書法

ngóhh séung máaih yāt-fūk bīu-hó-dīk jūng-gwok-syū-faat

Maps and guides

收銀檯 sāu-ngàhn-tòih	kiosk
週刊雜誌 jāu-hón-jaahp-ji	a weekly magazine
報紙　bo-jí	newspaper
地圖　deih-tòh	map

Do you have …	你們有 … néih-mùhn yáuh …
a map of the town?	本鎮的地圖嗎? bún-jan-dīk deih-tòh ma?
of the region?	地區的地圖嗎? deih-tòh mā?
Can you show me where … is on the map?	你能在地圖上為我指出 … 在哪裏嗎? néih nàhng joih deih-tòh-séuhng waih-ngóh jí-chūt … joih-náh-léih mā?

| Do you have a guidebook/a leaflet in English? | 你們有英文版的導遊册/小册子嗎?
néih-mùhn yáuh yīng-màhn-báan-dīk doh-yàuh-chaak/sīu-chaak-jí mā? |

Post office

. . . .

郵局 yáu-guhk	post office
郵票 yáuh-piu	stamps
挂號 gwa-hoh	registered
集邮者 jaahp-yàuh-jé	stamp collector
寄信/書 gei-sun/sūe	send a letter/book

| Where is the post office? | 郵局在哪裏?
yáu-guhk joih náh-léih? |

| When does it open? | 郵局甚麽時間開門?
yáu-guhk sahm-mō sìh-gāan hōi-mùhn? |

> **Asking the way** (p 36) > **Sightseeing** (p 96)

Which is the counter...?	哪個櫃檯 … ? náh-go gwaih-tòih … ?
for stamps	出售郵票 chūt-sauh yàuh-piu
for parcels	寄包裹 gei bāau-gwó
6 stamps for postcards...	六張寄明信片的郵票 luhk-jēung gei mìhng-seun-pin dīk yáu-piu
to Britain	寄往英國 gei-wóhng yīng-gwok
to America	寄往美國 gei-wóhng méih-gwok
I would like to send a letter to the UK.	我想寄信/書去英國 ngóhh-séung-gei-sun/ sūe-heui-yīng-gwok

How much extra does it cost to have it registered?

挂號要另付多少錢?

gwa-hoh yiu lihng-fooh dōh-síu-chình?

I am a stamp collector, I would like to buy the most recent stamps.

我是一名集邮者，我想買最新的郵票

ngóhh-sih yāt-mìngh-jaahp-yàuh-jé, ngóhh-séung-máaih jui-sān-dīk yàuh-piu

Can I send this parcel to the US by sea?

我能以海運的方式將這個包裹寄往美國嗎?

ngóhh nànhg yíh hói-wahn-dīk fōng-sīk jēung je-goh bāau-gwoh gei wóhng méih-gwok mā?

94

Photos

• •

A film for this camcorder

供這部錄像機使用的錄像帶

gung je-boh luhk-jeuhng-gēi sái-yuhng-dīk luhk-jeuhng-daai

Do you have batteries for this camera?

你們有這部相機使用的電池嗎?

néih-mùhn yáuh je-boh seung-gēi sái-yuhng-dīk dihn-chìh mā?

Leisure

Sightseeing and tourist office

Where is the tourist office?

游客服務處在哪裏?

yáu-haak-fuhk-mouh-chyu joih-náh-léih?

What can we visit in the area?

在這個地方我們可以參觀甚麼?

joih je-go mùhn-fōng ngóh-mùhn hó-yíh chāam-gūn sahm-mō?

Have you any leaflets?

你們有傳單嗎?

néih-mùhn yáuh chùehn-dāan mā?

Are there any excursions?

有哪些短程旅行嗎?

yáuh náh-sē dúen-chìhng leúih-hàhng mā?

96

We'd like to go to...	我們想去…
	ngóh-mùhn séung-heui...

How much does it cost to get in?	入門券要多少錢?
	yahp-mùn-huen yiu dō-síu-chìhn?

Are there reductions for...? children/ students/ over 60s	對兒童/學生/ 60歲以上的人仕有優惠價嗎?
	deui yìh-tùhng/hohk-sāang/ luhk-sáp-seui yíh-séuhng-dīk yàhn-sih yáuh yāu-waih-ga mā?

Entertainment

What is there to do in the evenings?	晚上有甚麼活動嗎?
	máahn-séuhng yáuh sahm-mō-wuht-duhng mā?

Do you have a programme of events?	你們有節目單嗎?
	néih-mùhn yáuh jit-muhk-dāan mā?

> **Maps and guides** (p 91)

| Is there anything for children? | 有甚麼孩子們可以參加的活動嗎?
yáuh sahm-mō hàaih-jí-mùhn hó-yíh chāam-gā-dīk wuht-duhng mā? |

Leisure/interests

• •

| Where can I/ we go...? | 我/我們去哪裏可以…?
ngóh/ngóh-mùhn heui náh-léih hó-yíh…? |

| fishing | 釣魚
diu-yùeh |

| walking | 步行
bouh-hàhng |

| Are there any good beaches near here? | 這附近有漂亮的沙灘嗎?
je fuh-gahn yáuh piu-leuhng-dīk sā-tāan mā? |

| Is there a swimming pool? | 有游泳池嗎?
yáuh yàuh-wihng-chìh mā? |

Music

歌劇　gōh-kehk	musical production
芭蕾舞　bā-lúih-móh	ballet
古典音樂會 gú-dín-yām-ngohk-wúi	classical music concert
現代音樂會 yihn-doih-yām-ngohk- wúi	modern music concert

I would like to
    see...

我想看…
ngóhh séung táai…

Are there any
    good concerts
    on?

有正在上演的好聽的音
樂會嗎?
yáuh jing-joih séuhng-yín-
    dīk hó-tēng-dīk yām-
    ngohk-wúi mā?

Where can I get tickets for the concert?	我在哪裏可以買音樂會的入場券? ngóh joih náh-léih hó-yíh máaih yām-ngohk-wúi-dīk yahp-chèuhng-huen?
Where can we hear some classical music/jazz?	我們去哪裏可以聽古典音樂/爵仕樂? ngóh-mùhn heui náh-léih hó-yíh tēng gú-dín-yām-ngohk/jeuk-sih-ngohk?

Cinema

What's on at the cinema (name of cinema) ...?	電影院現在正在上演甚麼電影? dihn-yíng-yúen yihn-joih jing-joih séuhng-yín sahm-mō dihn-yíng?
What time does the film start?	電影甚麼時間開演? dihn-yíng sahm-mō sìh-gāan hōi-yín?

> **Making friends** (p 26)

How much are the tickets?	電影票多少錢? dihn-yíng-piu dō-síu-chìhn?
Two for the (give time of perfomance) showing	買兩張正在上演的電影票 máaih léuhng-jēung jing-joih séuhng-yín-dīk dihn-yíng-piu

Theatre/opera

京劇 gīng-kehk	Peking/Beijing Opera
粵劇 yueht-kehk	Cantonese Opera
正廳前排 jing-tēng-chìhn-pàaih	stalls
半圓形摟座 bun-yùhn-yìhng-làuh-joh	circle
包廂 bāao-sēung	box
座位 joh-waih	seat
衣帽間 yī-moh-gāan	cloakroom

What is on at the theatre?	劇院正在上演甚麼戲劇？ kehk-yúen jing-joih séuhng-yín sahm-mō hei-kehk?
What prices are the tickets?	戲票多少錢？ hei-piu dō-síu-chìhn?
I'd like two tickets...	我想買兩張票… ngóh séung máaih léuhng-jēung piu…
for tonight	今晚的 gām-máahn-dīk
for tomorrow night	明晚的 mìhng-māan-dīk
for the 3rd of August	八月三號的 baat-yuht-sāam-hoh-dīk
When does the performance begin/end?	演出甚麼時間開始/ 結束？ yín-chūt sahm-mō sìh-gāan hōi-chí/git-chūk?

你不可以入去， 　因為演出已經開始了 néih ngh hó-yíh yahp- 　heui, yān-waih yín-chūt 　yíh-jīng hōi-chí-líuh	You can't go in, the performance has started
你在中間休息時可以 　入去 néih joih jūng-gāan 　yāu-sīk-sìh hó-yíh 　yahp-heui	You may enter at the interval

Television

遙控	yìuh-hung	remote control
開	hōi	to switch on
關	gwāan	to switch off
連續劇	lìhn-juhk-kehk	series/soap
新聞	sān-màhn	news
卡通片	kā-tūng-pin	cartoons

Where is the television?
電視機在哪裏?
dihn-sìh-gēi joih náh-léih?

How do you switch it on?
你怎麼打開電視?
néih jám-mō dá-hōi dihn-sìh?

What is on television?
有甚麼電視節目?
yáuh sahm-mō dihn-sìh-jit-muhk?

When is the news?	甚麼時間有新聞節目?
	sahm-mō sìh-gāan-yáuh sān-màhn-jit-muhk?

Do you have any English-language channels?	你們這裏有英文頻道嗎?
	néih-mùhn je-léih yāuh yīng-màhn-pàhn-doh mā?

Do you have any English videos?	你們這裏有英文錄像帶嗎?
	néih-mùhn je-léih yáuh yīng-màhn luhk-jeuhng-daai mā?

Sport

Where can we play...?	我們在哪裏可以玩…? ngóh-mùhn joih-náh-léih hó-yíh wàahn...?
Where can I/ we go...?	我/我們可以去哪裏…? ngóh/ngóh-mùhn hó-yíh heui náh-léih...?
swimming	游泳 yàuh-wihng
jogging	慢跑 maahn-páau
Do you have to be a member?	你必须是會員嗎? néih bīt-sēui sih wúi-yùhn mā?
How much is it per hour?	每小時多少錢? múih síu-sìh dō-síu-chìhn?

Leisure

Can we hire... rackets/golf clubs?	我們可以租借 ⋯ 球拍/高爾夫球棒嗎? ngóh-mùhn hó-yíh jō-je ... kàuh-paak/gōu-yíh-fùh- kàuh-páahng mā?
We'd like to see (name team) play	我們想看⋯隊的比賽 ngóh-mùhn séung tái ... deuih-dīk béi-choi
Where can I/we get tickets for the game?	我/我們在哪裏可以買這 場比賽的票? ngóh/ngóh-mùhn joih náh- léih hó-yíh máaih je- chèuhng béi-choi-dīk-piu?

YOU MAY HEAR...

這場比賽的票全賣 完了 je-chèuhng béi-choi-dīk piu chùehn-maaih- yùehn-líuh	There are no tickets left for the game

Walking

Are there any guided walks?	有導遊帶的步行活動嗎? yáuh doh-yàuh daai-dīk boh-hàhng-wuht-duhng mā?
Do you know any good walks?	你知道有好的步行活動嗎? néih ji-dou yáuh hó-dīk boh-hàhng-wuht-duhng mā?
How many kilometres is the walk?	這一步行活動要走多少公里? je-yāt boh-hàhng-wuht-duhng yiu-jáu dō-síu-gūng-léih?
Is it very steep?	很陡峭嗎? hán dáu-chiu mā?
How long will it take?	要花多長時間? yiu fā dō-chèuhng sì-gāan?

108

Is there a map of the walk?	有這一步行活動的地圖嗎？
	yáuh je-yāt boh-hàhng-wuht-duhng-dīk mùhn-tòh mā?
We'd like to go climbing	我們想去爬山
	ngóh-mùhn séung heui pàh-sāan
Do you have a detailed map of the area?	你們有該地區詳細的地圖嗎？
	néih-mùhn yáuh gōi mùhn-kūi chèuhng-sai-dīk mùhn-tòh mā?

> **Maps and guides** (p 91)

Communications

Telephone and mobile

. . . .

The international code for Hong Kong is 00 852. When you are calling Hong Kong from abroad, you dial 00 852 followed by an eight digit number. If you are calling within Hong Kong, you only need to dial the local eight digit number. If you are calling the UK from abroad, the UK international code is 00 44 plus the area code less the first 0.

When Chinese people make a phone call, they ask for the person they wish to speak to by name. It is not the Chinese caller's habit to give their own name first when making or receiving a call.

When giving telephone numbers, Chinese speakers normally read out the numbers one by one so that: 020 7900 0283 would be read:

零二零 七九零零 零二八三
lìhng yih lìhng chāt gáu lìhng lìhng lìhng yih
baat sāam

電話卡　dihn-wá-kāat	phonecard
手機　sáu-gēi	mobile
打電話　dá-dihn-wah	to make a phone call
電話號碼 dihn-wah-hoh-máh	phone number
分機號碼 fān-gēi-hoh-máh	extension number
本地電話 bún-deih-dihn-wá	local call
國內長途電話 gwok-noih-chèuhng- 　tòuh-dihn-wá	national call
國際長途電話 gwok-jai-chèuhng- 　tòuh-dihn-wá	international call

| I want to make a phone call | 我想打一個電話 |
| | ngóh séung dá yāt-go dihn-wá |

| Where can I buy a phonecard? | 我在哪裏能買一張電話卡? |
| | ngóh joih náh-léih nàhng máaih yāt-jēung dihn-wah-kāat? |

| A phonecard for ... yuan | 一張 ⋯ 圓的電話卡 |
| | yāt-jēung ... yùehn-dīk dihn-wah-kāat |

| Do you have a mobile? | 你有手機嗎? |
| | néih yāuh sáu-gēi mā? |

| What is your mobile number? | 請問你的手機號碼? |
| | chíng-mahn néih-dīk sáu-gēi-hoh-máh? |

| My mobile number is... | 我的手機號碼是⋯ |
| | ngóh-dīk sáu-gēi-hoh-máh sih... |

Mr Brown, please, 我要找布倫倫先生，
    extension... 　　　分機號碼…
            ngóh yiu jáau bo-lùhn sīn-

FACE TO FACE

A 你好
néih-hó
Hello

B 請叫 … 聽電話
chíng-giu … tīng dihn-wá
I'd like to speak to ..., please

A 請問你是誰?
chíng-mahn néih sih-sèuih?
Who's calling?

B 我是安琪拉
ngóh sih ōn-kèih-lāai
It's Angela

A 請等一等…
chíng dáng-yāt-dáng…
Just a moment...

Can I speak to...?	我能叫 ⋯ 聽電話嗎?
	ngóh nàhng giu ... tīng
	dihn-wá mā?

| Is that...? | 是 ⋯ 嗎? |
| | sih ... mā? |

| What is the code for ... ? | ⋯的區號是甚麼? |
| | ...dīk kūi hoh sih sahm mōh? |

| I'll call back in 5 minutes. | 我5分鐘後再打電話過來 |
| | ngóh ngh fān-jūng hauh joi dá dihn-wah gwoh lòih |

| Could you ask him to call me when he gets back? | 他回來時, 可否請他打電話給我? |
| | tā wòoih lòih sìh, hóh fáu chíng tā dā dihn wah kāp ngóh? |

| Sorry, I must have dialled the wrong number. | 對不起, 我撥錯電話號碼了 |
| | dùi ngh jueh, ngóhh booht choh dihn-wah hoh-máh-líuh |

We were cut off.	剛才電話斷線了
	gōng-chòih dihn-wa
	duehn-sin-líuh

| This is a very bad line. | 線路很不清楚 |
| | sin-lō hán bāt chīng-chóh |

I'll call back later	我一會再打過來
	ngóh yāt-wuih joi
	dá-gwo-lòih

I'll call back tomorrow	我明天再打過來
	ngóh-mìhng-tīn joi
	dá-gwo-lòih

This is Mr ... / Mrs ...	我是 … 先生/太太
	ngóh-sih … sīn-sāang/
	taai-taai

How do I get an outside line?	我如何撥打外線電話呢?
	ngóh yuèh-hòh buht-dá
	ngoih-sin-dihn-wá nē?

Please switch off all mobile phones	請關掉所有的手機
	chíng gwāan-diuh
	só-yáuh-dīk sáu-gēi

Telephone and mobile

我就是 ngóhh jauh sih	Speaking
請問你是誰? chíng mahn néih síh bīn waih?	Who's speaking?
請問你找誰? chíng mahn néih wàanh bīn waih?	Who would you like to speak to?
請稍候 chíng sáau hauh	Please hold (the line)
沒人接聽 mooht yành jip tēng	There's no reply
電話正在使用中 dihn-wá jing-joih sí-yuhng-jūng	The line is engaged
我能問你是誰嗎? ngóhh nàngh mahn néih sih bīn weih mā?	Who shall I say is calling?

我正在為你接通電話 ngóh jing-joih waih-néih jip-tūng dihn-wá	I'm trying to connect you
電話正忙，請過一會再打過來 dihn-wá jing-mòhng, chíng gwo yāt-wuih joi dá-gwo-lòih	The line is engaged, please try later
你想留言嗎? néih séung làuh-yìhn mā?	Do you want to leave a message?
···請在聽到信號後留言 ...chíng joih tīng-do sun-hoh-hauh láuh-yìhn	...leave a message after the tone

Telephone and mobile

117

Text messaging

．．．．．．．．．．．．．．．．．．．．．．．．．．．．．．．．．．．

I will text you | 我將發送信息給你
ngóh jēung faat-sung
sun-sīk kāp-néih

Can you text me? | 你能發送信息給我嗎?
néih nàhng faat-sung sun-sīk
kāp-ngóh mā?

Internet

．．．．．．．．．．．．．．．．．．．．．．．．．．．．．．．．．．．

Are there any
internet cafés
here? | 這裏有網吧嗎?
je-léih yáuh móhng-bā mā?

How much is it
to log on for
an hour? | 上網一個小時要付多少
錢?
séuhng-móhng yāt-go síu-sìh
yiu-fuh dō-síu-chìhn?

E-mail

∙∙∙∙∙∙∙∙∙∙∙∙∙∙∙∙∙∙∙∙∙∙∙∙∙∙∙∙∙∙∙∙∙∙∙∙∙∙∙

E-mail is very popular in Hong Kong; business
e-mails should be brief and not too familiar or
chatty.

New message	新信息	sān-sun-sīk
To	發給	faat-kāp
From	來自	lòih-jih
Subject	題目	tàih-muhk
cc	抄送	chāau-sung
bcc	隐蔽副本	yán-bai-fu-bún
Attachment	附件	fuh-gín
Send	發送	faat-sung

Do you have an e-mail?	你使用電子郵件嗎? néih sái-yuhng dihn-jí-yàuh-gín mā?

What is your e-mail address?	請問你的電子郵箱地址?
	chíng-mahn néih-dīk
	  dihn-jí-yàuh-sēung
	  mùhn-jí?

How do you spell it?	你如何拼寫這個字? néih yùeh-hòh ping-sé je-go jih?
All one word	這是一個字 je-sih yāt go jih
All lower case	全是小寫字母 chùehn-sih síu-sé jih-móh
My e-mail address is...	我的電子郵箱地址是… ngóh-dīk dihn-jí-yàuh-sēung deih-jí sih…

Can I send an e-mail?	我可以發送一封電子郵件嗎?
	ngóh hó-yíh faat-sung yāt-fūng dihn-jí-yàuh-gihn mā?

Did you get my e-mail?	你收到我的電子郵件了嗎?
	néih sāu-do ngóh-dīk dihn-jí-yàuh-gihn-líuh mā?

Fax

. . . .

The code for sending a fax to Hong Kong from the UK is 00 852 followed by an eight digit number. The code to fax the UK from Hong Kong is 00 44.

Addressing a fax

to	發給	faat-kāp
from	來自	lòih-jih
date	日期	yaht-kèih

please find attached	請閱附件	chíng-yueht-fuh-gín
a copy of...	一份 … 的副本	yāt-fahn … dīk-fu-bún
...pages in total	一共 … 頁	yāt-guhng … yihp
Do you have a fax?	你有傳真機嗎?	néih yáuh chùehn-jān-gēi mā?
I want to send a fax	我想發送一份傳真	ngóh séung faat-sung yāt-fahn chùehn-jān
What is your fax number?	請問你的傳真號碼?	chíng-mahn néih-dīk chùehn-jān-hoh-máh?
My fax number is...	我的傳真號碼是…	ngóh-dīk chùehn-jān-hoh-máh sih…

Practicalities

Money

• •

The Hong Kong Dollar (góng-baih) is the currency in Hong Kong. The units of góng-baih are known as dollars (māan) and cents (sīn).

信用卡 sun-yuhng-kāat	credit card
提款機　tàih-fún-gēi	cash dispenser
收據　　sāu-geui	till receipt

Where can I change some money?	我在哪裏可以換錢? ngóh joih náh-léih hó-yíh 　wuhn-chìhn?
When does the bank open?	銀行甚麼時間開門? ngàhn-hàhng sahm-mō 　sìh-gāan hōi-mùhn?

Money

123

| When does the bank close? | 銀行甚麼時間關門? |
| | ngàhn-hàhng sahm-mō sìh-gāan gwāan-mùhn? |

| Can I pay with ... euros/Swiss francs? | 我可以用 ··· 歐圓/瑞士法郎付款嗎? |
| | ngóh hó-yíh yuhng ... āu-yùehn/suih-sih faat-lòhng fuh-fún mā? |

| I want to change these traveller's cheques | 我想兌現這些旅行支票 |
| | ngóh séung deuih-yihn je-sē lúih-hàhng-jī-piu |

| Where is the nearest cash dispenser? | 離這裏最近的提款機在哪裏? |
| | lèih je-léuih jeui-gahn-dīk tàih-fún-gēi joih náh léuih? |

| Can I use my credit card at the cash dispenser? | 我可以使用信用卡從提款機提款嗎? |
| | ngóh hó-yíh sí-yuhng seun-yuhng-kāat chùhng tàih-fún-gēi tàih-fún mā? |

Practicalities

Do you have any loose change?	你有零錢嗎?
	néih yáuh lìhng-chìhn mā?

Paying

How much is it?	多少錢?
	dō-síu chìhn?

How much will it be?	要付多少錢?
	yiu fuh- dō-síu chìhn?

Can I pay by ... credit card/ cheque?	我可以使用 ⋯ 信用卡/支票付款嗎?
	ngóh hó-yíh sái-yuhng ...
	sun-yuhng-kāat/jī-piu
	fuh-fún mā?

Is service included?	服務費已經包括在內了 嗎?
	fuhk-moh-fai yíh-gīng
	bāau-kut joih-noih-líuh mā?

Put it on my bill	請加在我的帳單上 chíng gā joih ngóh-dīk jeung-dāan séuhng
Where do I pay?	我在哪裏付款? ngóh joih náh-léih fuh-fún?
I need a receipt, please	請給我一張收據 chíng kāp-ngóh yāt-jēung sāu-geui
Do I pay in advance?	我需要預先付款嗎? ngóh sēi-yiu yuehn-sīn fuh-fún mā?
Do I need to pay a deposit?	我需要先付定金嗎? ngóh sēui-yiu sīn-fuh dihng-gām mā?
I'm sorry	對不起 dui-ngh jueh
I've nothing smaller (no change)	我没有零錢 ngóh mòh lìhng-chìhn

服務費已包括在內，但没包括小費 fohk-moh-fai yíh bāau-kut-joih-noih, daahn-mòh-bāau-kut síu-fai	Service is included but not a tip
在收銀處付款 joih sāu-ngàhn-chyu fuh-fún	Pay at the till

Luggage

領取行李 líhng-chéui-háhng-léih	baggage reclaim
行李房 hàhng-léih fòhng	left-luggage office
行李推車 hàhng-léih-tūi-chē	luggage trolley

Luggage

> **Shopping phrases** (p 76)

| My luggage hasn't arrived | 我的行李還没到
ngóh-dīk hàhng-léih juhng-mei-dóh |
| My suitcase has been damaged on the flight | 我的行李箱在飛行中損壞了
ngóh-dīk hàhng-léih-sēung joih fēi-hàhng-jūng súen-waaih-líuh |

Repairs

This is broken	這壞了 je waaih-líuh
Where can I have this repaired?	我在哪裏可以把它修理好? ngóh joih náh-léih hó-yíh bá-tā sāu-léih-hó?
Is it worth repairing?	值得把它修好嗎? jihk-dāk bá-tā sāu-léih-hó mā?

Practicalities

Can you repair...?	你能修理 … 嗎?
	néih nàhng sāu-léih … mā?
this	這件東西
	je-gihn dūng-sāi
these shoes	這些鞋子
	je-sē hàaih-jí
my watch	我的手錶
	ngóh-dīk sáu-bīu

YOU MAY HEAR...

對不起, 但是我們無法修好它 dui-ngh-jueh, daahn-sih ngóh-mùhn mòh-faat sāu-hó tā	Sorry, but we can't mend it

Laundry

乾洗店	gōn-sái-dim	dry-cleaner's
洗衣粉	sái-yī-fán	soap powder
去污液	heui-wū-yihk	bleach
洗衣機	sái-yī-gēi	washing machine

Where can I wash these clothes?

我在哪裏可以洗這些衣服?

ngóh joih náh-léih hó-yíh sái je-sē yī-fuhk?

Where is the nearest launderette?

離這裏最近的乾洗店在哪裏?

lèih je-léih jeui-gahn-dīk gōn-sái-dim joih náh-léih?

Complaints

● ●

This does not work/It's broken	這壞了 je waaih-líuh
It's dirty	這很髒 je hán-jōng
light	燈 dāng
toilet	厠所 chi-sóh
heating	暖氣 núehn-hei
air conditioning	空調 hūng-tìuh
I want a refund	我要退款 ngóh yiu teui-fún

> **Hotel (desk)** (p 71)

Complaints

Problems

Can you help me?	你能幫助我嗎? néih nàhng bōng-joh ngóh mā?
I speak very little Cantonese	我只會說一點點廣東話 ngóh ji wúih suet yāt-dím-dím gwóng-dūng-wah
Does anyone here speak English?	這裏有人會說英文嗎? je-léih yáuh-yàhn wúih suet yīng-màhn mā?
What's the matter?	甚麼事? sahm-mō sìh?
I would like to speak to whoever is in charge of...	我想和負责 … 的人談談 ngóh séung wòhk fuh-jaak … dīk-yàhn góng-góng
I'm lost	我迷路了 ngóh màih-louh-líuh

Practicalities

| How do you get to...? | 你怎麼去 ⋯ 呢? |
| | néih-jám-mōh-hui ... nē? |

| I missed my train | 我錯過了火車 |
| | ngáh chóhk-gwo-líuh fó-chē |

| plane | 飛機 |
| | fēi-gēi |

| connection | 中轉 |
| | jūng-juen |

| The coach has left without me | 長途客車沒等我就開走了 |
| | chèuhng-tòh haak-chē muht-dáng ngóh-jauh hōi-jáu-líuh |

| Can you show me how this works, please? | 你能向我展示怎麼使用這件東西嗎? |
| | néih nàhng heung-ngóh jín-sih jám-mō sái-yuhng je-gihn dūng-sāi mā? |

| I have lost my money | 我丟了錢 |
| | ngóh dīu-líuh chìhn |

> **Hotel desk** (p 71)

I need to get to...	我需要到達… ngóh sēui-yiu do-daaht...
I need to get in touch with the British consulate	我需要聯絡英國領事館 ngóh sēui-yiu lùehn-lok yīng-gwok-líhng-sih-góon
Leave me alone!	別打擾我！ bít-dá-yíuh ngóh!
Go away!	走開！ jáu-hō!

Emergencies

In China, you ring 120 to call an ambulance, 999 to call the fire brigade and 110 to call the police.

救護車 gau-wuh-chē	ambulance
軍警 gwān-gíng	military police
警察 gíng-chaat	police

消防員 sīu-fòhng-yùehn	firemen
消防隊 sīu-fòhng-duih	fire brigade
警察局 gíng-chaat-guhk	police station
着火 jeuhk-huo	on fire
碰撞 pung-johng	crash

Help!	救命啊! gau-mehng-a!
Fire!	着火了! jeuhk-fó-líuh!
Can you help me?	你能幫助我嗎? néih nàhng bōng-joh ngóh mā?
There's been an accident!	出事故了! chūt-sih-gu-líuh!

Emergencies

Someone ... has been injured/ has been knocked down	有人 … 受傷了/ 被撞倒了 yáuh-yàhn … sauh-sēung-líuh/beih-johng-dóu-líuh
My car crashed	我撞了車 ngóhh johng-líuh-chē
I have crashed my car on the motorway	我在高速公路上撞了車 ngóhh-joih-gō-chūk-gūng-loh-séungh-johng-líuh-chē
Please call ... the police/ an ambulance	請叫 … 警察/救護車 chíng-giu...gíng-chaat/gau-wuh-chē
Where is the police station?	警察局在哪裏? gíng-chaat-guhk joih náh-léih?
I want to report a crime	我要報案 ngóh yiu bo-on
I've been ... robbed/attacked	我被 … 搶了/毆打了 ngóh-beih … chéung-líuh/áu-dá-líuh

Someone's stolen ... my bag/ traveller's cheques	某人偷了 … 我的袋/ 旅行支票	máuh-yàhn tāu-líuh … ngóh-dīk doih/ lúih-hàhng-jī-piu
A thief has stolen my purse	扒手偷了我的錢包	pàh-sáu tāu-líuh ngóh-dīk chìhn-bāau
My car has been stolen	我的車被盜了	ngóh-dīk chē beih-doh-líuh
I've been raped	我被人強姦了	ngóh beih-yàhn kèuhg-gāan-líuh
I want to speak to a policewoman	我想和一名女警員談話	ngóh séung wòh yāt-mìhng néuih-gíng-yùehn tàahm-wah
I need to make a telephone call	我需要打個電話	ngóh sēui-yiu dá-go dihn-wá

Emergencies

I need a report for my insurance	我需要一份報告給保險公司
	ngóh sēui-yiu yāt-fahn bo-go kāp bó-hím-gūng-sī
I didn't know there was a speed limit	我當時不知道有時速限制
	ngóh dōng-sìh ngh-jī-dóh yáuh sìh-chūk-haahn-jai
How much is the fine?	罰錢多少?
	faht-chìhn dō-síu?
Where do I pay it?	我在哪裏付款?
	Ngóh joih náh-léih fuh-fún?
Do I have to pay it straightaway?	我需要馬上付款嗎?
	ngóh sēui-yiu máh-seuhng fuh-fún mā?
I'm very sorry, officer	我很抱歉, 警官
	ngóh hán-póh-hip, gíng-gūn

Health

Pharmacy

藥劑師 yeuhk-jāi-sī	pharmacy/chemist
值班藥劑師 jihk-bāan yeuhk-jāi-sī	duty chemist

Can you give me
  something for...?

你能給我…嗎?
néih nàhng kāp ngóh…mā?

a headache
頭痛
tàuh-tung

car sickness
暈車
wàhn-chē

a cough
咳嗽
kāt-sau

diarrhoea	肚痛的藥 tóh-tung-dīk-yeuhk
Is it safe for children?	孩子吃這種藥安全嗎? hàaih-jí sik je-júng-yeuhk ōn-chùehn mā?
How much should I give him?	我應該給他服用多少劑 量? ngóh yīng-gōi kāp-tā fuhk yuhng dō-síu jāi-leuhng?

YOU MAY HEAR...	
每日三次… múih-yaht sāam-chi…	Three times a day...
在吃飯之前/ 在吃飯時/ 在吃飯之後 joih hek-faahn ji-chìhn/ joih hek-faahn sìh/joih hek-faahn ji-hauh	before/with/after ...meals

Health

Doctor

醫院　yī-yúen	hospital
急診室　gāp-chán-sāt	casualty
當地健康中心 dōng-deih-gihn- 　hōng-jūng-sām	local health centre
呼吸困難 fōo-kàph-kwan-nàanh	breathing difficulties
心臟病 sām-johng-behng	heart disease
心跳　sām-tiu	heartbeat
高/低血壓 gō/dāi-huet-aat	high/low blood pressure
糖尿病 tòngh-niuh-behng	diabetes
貧血症 pành-huet-jing	anaemia

A 我生病了
ngóh sāang-behng-líuh
I feel ill

B 你發燒嗎?
néih faat-sīu mā?
Do you have a temperature?

A 我這裏痛⋯
bāt, ngóh je-léih tung…
No, I have a pain here...

I need a doctor	我需要看醫生	
	ngóh sēui-yiu tái yī-sāang	
My son is ill	我的兒子生病了	
	ngóh-dīk yìh-jí	
	sāang-behng-líuh	
My daughter is ill	我的女兒生病了	
	ngóh-dīk núih-yìh	
	sāang-behng-líuh	

I'm diabetic	我患有糖尿病
	ngóh waahn-yáuh
	tòhng-niuh-behng

| I'm pregnant | 我怀孕了 |
| | ngóh wàaih-yahn-líuh |

I'm on the pill	我一直在吃避孕藥
	ngóh yāt-jihk joih sihk
	beih-yahn-yeuhk

I'm allergic to penicillin	我對盤尼西林過敏
	ngóh deui pùhn-nèih-sāi-lāhm
	gwo-máhn

I am having breathing difficulties at the moment	我現在呼吸困難
	ngóh yihn-joih fōo-kàph
	kwan-nàanh

I have been suffering from heart disease for a long time	我長期患有心臟病
	ngóh chèungh-kèih
	waahn-yáuh sām-johng-
	behng

143

My heart is beating very fast at the moment	我現在心跳很快 ngóh yihn-joih sām-tiu hán-faai
I have been suffering from high/low blood pressure for years	我多年以來一直患有高/低血壓 ngóh dōh-nình-lòih yāt-jihk waahn-yáuh gō/dāi huet-aat
I am anaemic	我患有貧血症 ngóh waahn-yáuh pành-huet-jing
Will he/she have to go to hospital?	他/她要去醫院嗎? tā/tā yiu heui yī-yúen mā?
When are the visiting hours?	探病時間是甚麼時候? taam-behng sìh-gāan sih sahm-mō sìh-hauh?
Will I have to pay?	我必須付錢嗎? ngóh bīt-sēui- fuh-chìhn mā?

| How much will it cost? | 要多少錢?
yiu dō-síu chìhn? |
| Can you give me a receipt for the insurance? | 你能給我一張保險公司要的收據嗎?
néih nàhng kāp ngóh yāt-jēung bó-hím-gūng-sī yiu-dīk sāu-gēui mā? |

你必须去醫院 néih bīt-sēui heui yī-yúen	You will have to go to hospital
不嚴重 ngh-yìhm-chúhng	It's not serious

Doctor

> **Emergencies** (p 134)

145

Dentist

● ●

| I need a dentist | 我需要看牙醫 |
| | ngóh sēui-yiu tái ngàh-yī |

| He/She has toothache | 他/她牙痛 |
| | tā/tā ngàh-tung |

| Can you do a temporary filling? | 你能做臨時的補牙嗎? |
| | néih nàhng joh làhm-sìh-dīk bó-ngàh mā? |

| It hurts | 痛 |
| | tung |

| Can you give me something for the pain? | 你能給我一些止痛藥嗎? |
| | néih nàhng kāp ngóh yāt-sē jí-tung-yuehk mā? |

| Can you repair my dentures? | 你能補我的假牙嗎? |
| | néih nàhng bó ngóh-dīk gá-ngàh mā? |

| Do I have to pay? | 我要付錢嗎? |
| | ngóh yiu fuh-chìhn mā? |

| How much will it be? | 要多少錢? |
| | yiu dō-síu-chìhn? |

| Can I have a receipt for my insurance? | 你能給我一張保險公司要的收據嗎? |
| | néih nàhng kāp ngóh yāt-jēung bó-hím-gūng-sī yiu-dīk sāu-gēui mā? |

YOU MAY HEAR...

我必须把它拔出來 ngóh bīt-sūi bá-tā baht chūt-lòih	I'll have to take it out
你需要補一顆牙 néih sēui-yiu bó yāt-fó ngàh	You need a filling
可能會有些痛 hó-nàhng wuih yáuh-sē tung	This might hurt a little

Dentist

Different types of travellers

Disabled travellers

What facilities do you have for disabled people?	你們這裏有哪些為殘疾人仕提供的設施？ néih-mùhn je-léih yáuh náh-sē waih chàahn-jaht-yàhn-sih tàih-gūung-dīk chit-sī?
Are there any toilets for the disabled?	有供殘疾人仕使用的廁所嗎？ yáuh gūng chàahn-jaht-yàhn-sih sái-yuhng-dīk chi-só mā?
Do you have any bedrooms on the ground floor?	你們這裏有在一樓的臥室嗎？ néih-mùhn je-léih yáuh joih yāt-láu-dīk ngoh-sāt mā?

148

Is there a lift?	有電梯嗎?
	yáuh dihn-tāi mā?
Where is the lift?	電梯在哪裏?
	dihn-tāi joih náh-léih?
Can you visit ... in a wheelchair?	坐輪椅的人仕能去參觀 ⋯ 嗎?
	chóh lùhn-yí-dīk yàhn-sih nàhng heui chāam-gūn ... mā?
Do you have wheelchairs?	你們有輪椅嗎?
	néih-mùhn yáuh lùhn-yí mā?
Where is the wheelchair-accessible entrance?	輪椅可以進入的入口在 哪裏?
	lùhn-yí hó-yíh jun-yahp-dīk yahp-háu joih-náh-léih?
Do you have an induction loop?	你們有介紹課嗎?
	néih-mùhn yáuh gaai-siuh-fo mā?
Is there a reduction for disabled people?	殘疾人仕有優惠價嗎?
	chàahn-jaht-yàhn-sih yáuh yāu-waih-ga mā?

| Is there somewhere I can sit down? | 我在哪裏能坐下來?
ngóh joih náh-léih nàhng chóh-lohk-lòih? |

With kids

A child's ticket	兒童票 yìh-tùhng-piu
He/She is ... years old	他/她 ⋯ 歲了 tā/tā ... seui-líuh
Is there a reduction for children?	兒童有優惠價嗎? yìh-tùhng yáuh yāu-waih-gaai mā?
Do you have a children's menu?	你們有小朋友的菜單嗎? néih-mùhn yáuh síu-pàhng-yáuh-dīk choi-dāan mā?
Is it OK to take children?	帶小朋友來可以嗎? daai síu-pàhng-yáuh lòih hó-yíh mā?

> **Hotel** (p 67)

Do you have … a high chair/ a cot?	你們有 ⋯ 兒童高椅子/ 兒童床嗎?
	néih-mùhn yáuh … yìh-tùhng gō-yí-jí/yìh-tùhng-chòhng mā?
I have two children	我有两個孩子
	ngóh yáuh léuhng-go hàaih-jí
He/She is 8 years old	他/她八歲了
	tā/tā baat-seui-líuh
Do you have any children?	你有孩子嗎?
	néih yáuh hàaih-jí mā?

With kids

> **Pharmacy** (p 139) > **Doctor** (p 141)

Reference

Measurements and quantities

....

1 斤 (jān) = 0.5 kilo

Liquids 液体

....

1/2 litre of...	半升··· bun-sīng...
a litre of...	一升··· yāt-sīng...
1/2 bottle of...	半瓶··· bun-pìhng...
a bottle of...	一瓶··· yāt-pìhng...
a glass of...	一杯··· yāt-būi...

Weights 重量

| 100 grams | 100克 |
| | yāt-baak-hāk |

| 1/2 kilo of... | 半公斤··· |
| | boon-gūng-gān... |

| a kilo of... | 一公斤··· |
| | yāt-gūng-jān... |

Food 食品

| a slice of... | 一片··· |
| | yāt-pin... |

| a portion of... | 一份··· |
| | yāt-fahn... |

| a dozen... | 十二個··· |
| | sahp-yih-go... |

| a box of... | 一盒··· |
| | yāt-hahp... |

| a packet of... | 一包… |
| | yāt-bāau… |

| a tin of... | 一罐… |
| | yāt-gun… |

| a can of... (beer) | 一罐 … （啤酒） |
| | yāt-gun … (bē-jáu) |

Miscellaneous 其它杂物

| …yuan worth of... | …圓的… |
| | …yùehn-dīk… |

| a quarter | 四分之一 |
| | sei-fahn-ji-yāt |

| 20 per cent | 百分之二十 |
| | baak-fahn-ji-yih-sahp |

| more than... | 多於… |
| | dō-yū… |

| less than... | 少於… |
| | síu-yū… |

| double | 两倍 |
| | léuhng-púih |

Numbers

0	零	lìhng	LING
1	一	yāt	
2	二	yih	YEE
3	三	sāam	SAM
4	四	sei	SAY
5	五	ńgh	
6	六	luhk	LOCK ?
7	七	chāt	
8	八	baat	BAT
9	九	gáu	GOW
10	十	sahp	SUP
11	十一	sahp-yāt	
12	十二	sahp-yih	

13	十三	sahp-sāam
14	十四	sahp-sei
15	十五	sahp-ńgh
16	十六	sahp-luhk
17	十七	sahp-chāt
18	十八	sahp-baat
19	十九	sahp-gáu
20	二十	yih-sahp
21	二十一	yih-sahp-yāt
22	二十二	yih-sahp-yih
23	二十三	yih-sahp-sāam
24	二十四	yih-sahp-sei
25	二十五	yih -sahp-ńgh
26	二十六	yih-sahp-luhk
27	二十七	yih-sahp-chāt
28	二十八	yih-sahp-baat
29	二十九	yih-sahp-gáu

30	三十	sāam-sahp
40	四十	sei-sahp
50	五十	ńgh-sahp
60	六十	luhk-sahp
70	七十	chāt-sahp
80	八十	baat-sahp
90	九十	gáu-sahp
100	一百	yāt-baak
110	一百一十	yāt-baak-yāt-sahp
1000	一千	yāt-chīn
2000	两千	léuhng-chīn
million	一百万	yāt-baak-maahn
billion	十亿	sahp-yīk

1st	第一 daih-yāt	2nd	第二 daih-yih
3rd	第三 daih-sāam	4th	第四 daih-sei

5th	第五 daih-ńgh	6th	第六 daih-luhk
7th	第七 daih-chāt	8th	第八 daih-baat
9th	第九 daih-gáu	10th	第十 daih-sahp

15th	第十五	daih-sahp-ńgh
20th	第二十	daih-yih-sahp
50th	第五十	daih-ńgh-sahp
100th	第一百	daih-yāt-baak
101st	第一百零一	daih-yāt-baak-lìhng-yāt
110th	第一百一十	daih-yāt-baak-yāt-sahp
1,000th	第一千	daih-yāt-chīn

Fractions and percentages

½	二分之一	yih-fān-jī-yāt
⅓	三分之一	sāam-fān-jī-yāt
¼	四分之一	sei-fān-jī-yāt
⅔	三分之二	sāam-fān-jī-yih
0.5	零點五	lìhng-dím-ńgh
3.5	三點五	sāam-dím-ńgh
6.89	六點八九	luhk-dím-baat-gáu
10%	百分之十	báak-fān-jī-sahp
100%	百分之百	báak-fān-jī-báakh

Numbers

> **Emergencies** (p 134) > **Sport** (p 106)

Days and months

Days 日

Monday	星期一	sīng-kèih-yāt
Tuesday	星期二	sīng-kèih-yih
Wednesday	星期三	sīng-kèih-sāam
Thursday	星期四	sīng-kèih-sei
Friday	星期五	sīng-kèih-ńgh
Saturday	星期六	sīng-kèih-luhk
Sunday	星期日	sīng-kèih-yaht

Seasons 季节

spring	春天	chūn-tīn
summer	夏天	hah-tīn
autumn	秋天	chāu-tīn
winter	冬天	dūng-tīn

Months 月

January	一月	yāt-yueht
February	二月	yih-yueht
March	三月	sāam-yueht
April	四月	sei-yueht
May	五月	ńgh-yueht
June	六月	luhk-yueht
July	七月	chāt-yueht
August	八月	baat-yueht
September	九月	gáu-yueht
October	十月	sahp-yueht
November	十一月	sahp-yāt-yueht
December	十二月	sahp-yih-yueht

| What is today's date? | 今天是幾月幾日?
gām-tīn sih
géi-yueht-géi-yaht? |
| What day is it today? | 今天是星期幾?
gām-tīn sih sīng-kèih-géi? |

Today is the 5th of March 2007	今天是2007年3月5日 gām-tīn sih yih-lìhng-lìhng-chāt-nìhn sāam-yueht-ńgh-yaht

在20日 joih yih sahp yaht	on the 20th
1月1日 yāt yueht yāt yaht	the first of January
在2007年 joih yih lìhng lìhng chāt nìhn	in 2007
在十九世纪 joih sahp gáu sai-géi	in the nineteenth century
在九十年代 joih gáu sahp nình-doih	in the Nineties

on Saturday	在星期六 joih sīng-kèih-luhk
every Saturday	每逢星期六 múih-fùhng sīng-kèih-luhk

this Saturday	本星期六	bún sīng-kèih-luhk
next Saturday	下星期六	hah sīng-kèih-luhk
last Saturday	上星期六	séuhng sīng-kèih-luhk
in June	在六月份	joih luhk-yueht-fàhn
at the beginning of June	在六月初	joih luhk-yueht-chōh
at the end of June	在六月末	joih luhk-yueht-muht
before summer	夏天之前	hah-tīn ji-chìhn
during the summer	夏季	hah-gwai
after summer	夏天之後	hah-tīn ji-hauh

Time

....

What time is it, please?	請問現在幾點了? chíng-mahn yihn-joih géi-dím-líuh?
It's ...	現在是 … yihn-joih sih …
2 o'clock	兩點鐘 léuhng-dím-jūng
3 o'clock	三點鐘 sāam-dím-jūng
6 o'clock (etc.)	六點鐘 luhk-dím-jūng
1 o'clock	現在是一點鐘 yihn-joih sih yāt-dím-jūng
It's midday	現在是中午十二點鐘 yihn-joih sih jūng-ńgh sahp-yih-dím-jūng

It's midnight	現在是半夜十二點鐘
	yihn-joih sih bun-yeh
	sahp-yih-dím-jūng

| 9 | 九點 |
| | gáu-dím |

| 9.10 | 九點十分 |
| | gáu-dím-sahp-fān |

| quarter past 9 | 九點一刻 |
| | gáu-dím-yāt-hāk |

| 9.20 | 九點二十分 |
| | gāu-dím-yih-sahp-fān |

| 9.30 | 九點半 |
| | gāu-dím-bun |

| 9.35 | 九點三十五分 |
| | gáu-dím-sāam-sahp-ńgh-fān |

| quarter to 10 | 九點四十五分 |
| | gáu-dím-sei-sahp-ńgh-fān |

| 5 to 10 | 十點五分 |
| | sahp-dím-ńgh-fān |

Time phrases

When does it open/close?	甚麼時間開門/關門? sahm-mō sìh-gāan hōi-mùhn/ gwāan-mùhn?
When does it begin/finish?	甚麼時間開始/结束? sahm-mō sìh-gāan hōi-chí/ git-chūk?
at 3 o'clock	三點 sāam-dím
before 3 o'clock	三點之前 sāam-dím-ji-chìhn
after 3 o'clock	三點之後 sāam-dím-ji-hauh
today	今天 gām-tīn
tonight	今晚 gām-máahn

Reference

tomorrow	明天 mìhng-tīn
yesterday	昨天 johk-tīn

前天 chình-tīn	the day before yesterday
后天 hauh-tīn	the day after tomorrow
昨天上午/下午/晚上 johk-tīn séungh ńgh/hah ńgh/máanh séungh	yesterday morning/afternoon/evening
明天上午/下午/晚上 mìngh tīn séungh ńgh/hah ńgh/máanh séungh	tomorrow morning/afternoon/evening
第二天 dīk yih tīn	the next day

Eating out

In a bar/café

FACE TO FACE

A 你想飲甚麼?
néih- séung yám-sahm-mō?
What would you like to drink?

B 茶, 謝謝
chàh, jeh-jeh
Tea please

a coffee	一杯咖啡
	yāt-būi ga-fē
a beer	一支啤酒
	yāt-jī bē-jáu

an orange juice	一杯橙汁
	yāt-būi cháang-jāp
with lemon	加檸檬
	gā nìhng-mūng
no sugar	不加糖
	ngh-gā tòhng
for two	要兩份
	yiu léuhng-fahn
for me	給我
	kāp-ngóh
for him/her	給他/她
	kāp-tā/tā
for us	給我們
	kāp-ngóh-mùhn
with ice	加冰
	gā-bīng

a bottle of mineral water	一瓶礦泉水	yāt-pìhng kwong-chùehn-séui
sparkling	有汽泡的	yáuh hei-pāau-dīk
still	無汽泡的	mòh hei-pāau-dīk

At the teahouse

中國茶 jūng-gwok-chàh	Chinese tea
紅/綠茶 hùhng/luhk-chàh	red/green tea
一壺茶 yāt-wòoh-chàh	a pot of tea
滾水 gwán-súi	boiled water
苦 fóo	bitter
小費 síu-fai	tip (for service)

| I would like to drink Chinese red/green tea | 我想飲中國紅/綠茶 |
| | ngóhh séung yám jūng-gwok-hùhng/luhk-chàh |

| How much is a pot of tea? | 請問一壺茶多少錢? |
| | chíng-mahn yāt-wòoh-chàh dōh-síu-chình? |

| Please add more boiled water | 請加滾水 |
| | chíng-gā gwán-súi |

| This kind of tea is too bitter | 這種茶太苦了 |
| | je-júng-chàh taai-fóo-líuh |

| This is your tip, thanks | 這是給你的小費,謝謝 |
| | je-sih kāp néih dīk síu-fai, jeh-jeh |

| 你想飲哪種中國茶? | What kind of Chinese tea would you like to drink? |
| néih séung yám náh-júng jūng-gwok-chàh? | |

What is the dish of the day?	今天有甚麼招牌菜? gām-tīn yáuh sahm-mō jīu-pàaih-choi?
Do you have a tourist menu?	你們有為遊客準備的菜單嗎? néih-mùhn yáuh waih yàuh-haak jéun-beih-dīk choi-dāan mā?
At a set price?	價錢固定的菜單嗎? gaai-chìhn gu-dihng-dīk choi-dāan mā?
What is the speciality of the house?	這裏的招牌菜是甚麼? je-léih-dīk jīu-pàaih-choi sih sahm-mō?
Can you tell me what this is?	請告訴我這是甚麼菜? chíng go-so ngóh je sih sahm-mō choi?
I'll have this	我要點這道菜 ngóh yiu dím je doh-choi

Could we have a bottle of mineral water, please?	請再給我們拿一瓶礦泉水好嗎?
	chíng joi kāp ngóh-mùhn nàh yāt-pìhng kwong-chùehn-séui hó-mā?
The bill, please	我要埋單
	ngóh yiu màaih-dāan,
Is service included?	服務費已包括在內了嗎?
	fuhk-moh-fai yíh bāau-kut joih-nòih-líuh mā?

In a restaurant

●●

FACE TO FACE

A 我想預定一張 … 人的檯
ngóh-séung yueh-dihng yāt-jāung …
   yàhn-dīk-tòih
I'd like to book a table for ... people

B 好, 甚麼時間的?
hó, sahm-mō sìh-gāan-dīk?
Yes, when for?

A 今晚…/明晚…/八點
gām-maáhn.../mìhng-máahn.../baat-dím
Tonight.../for tomorrow night.../at 8 o'clock

The menu, please 請拿菜單給我
                 chíng ló choi-dāan kāp-ngóh

Vegetarian

Are there any vegetarian restaurants here?	這裏有素菜飯館嗎?	je-léih yáuh jāai-choi faahn-gún mā?
Do you have any vegetarian dishes?	你們這裏有素菜嗎?	néih-mùhn je-léih yáuh jāai-choi mā?
Which dishes have no meat/fish?	哪些菜裏没有肉/魚?	náh-sē choi léih mòh yuhk/ yùh?
What fish dishes do you have	你們有哪些魚?	néih-mùhn yáuh náh-sē yùh?
I don't like meat	我不喜歡吃肉	ngóh ngh-héi-fūn sīk-yuhk
What do you recommend?	你能建議我點些甚麼菜嗎?	néih-nàhng gin-yíh ngóh dím-sē sahm-mō choi mā?

Wines and spirits

白蘭地 baahk-làahn-deih	brandy
威仕忌　wāi-sih-géi	whisky
茅檯酒 màauh-tòih-jāu	famous Chinese rice wine called 'Maotai', quite strong
二鍋頭　yih-wō-tàuh	well-known Chinese rice wines, quite strong
女兒紅 núih-yìh-hùhng	well-known Chinese rice wines

The wine list, please	請拿酒單給我	chíng lók jáu-dāan kāp-ngóh
white wine	白葡萄酒	baahk pàh-tòh-jáu

| red wine | 紅葡萄酒 |
| | hùhng pòh-tòh-jáu |

| Can you recommend a good local wine? | 你能建議好飲的當地葡萄酒嗎? |
| | néih nàhng gin-yíh hó-yám-dīk dōng-deih pòh-tòh-jáu mā? |

| A bottle... | 一瓶··· |
| | yāt-pìhng... |

| A carafe... | 一玻璃瓶的··· |
| | yāt-bóh-lēih-pìhng-dīk... |

| What liqueurs do you have? | 你們有哪些烈酒? |
| | néih-mùhn yáuh náh-sē liht-jáu? |

Menu reader

Soft drinks

七喜 chāt–héi Lemonade

中國绿茶 jūng–gwok luhk–chàh
Chinese green tea

鲜榨橙汁 sīn–ja cháang–jāp
Freshly squeezed orange juice

Beers

青岛啤酒 chēng–dó bē–jāu
Qingdao beer

珠江啤酒 jyū–gōng bē–jáu
Zhujiang beer

燕京啤酒 yin–gīng bē–jáu
Yanjing beer

Wines

長城牌白葡萄酒 chèuhng-sìhng-pàaih
baahk pòh-tàh-jáu Changcheng white wine

長城牌紅葡萄酒 chèuhng-sìhng-pàaih
hùhng pòh-tàh-jáu Changcheng red wine

Spirits and liqueurs

茅檯酒 màauh-tòih-jáu Maotai rice wine

女兒紅 núih-yìh-hùhng Nuierhong rice wine

二鍋頭 yih-wō-tàuh Erguotou rice wine

Soups

豆腐雜菜湯 dauh-fuh jaahp-choi tōng
Tofu/bean curd and mixed vegetable soup

雞蛋番茄湯 gāi-daahn fāan-kèh tōng
Egg and tomato soup

雞粒玉米羹 gāi-nāp yueh-máih gāng
Diced chicken and sweetcorn soup

Menu reader

雞肉蘑菇湯 gāi-yuhk mòh-gū tōng
Chicken and mushroom soup

酸辣湯 sūen-laaht tōng Hot and sour soup

魚片豆腐湯 yùeh-pin dauh-fóo tōng
Shredded fish and tofu/bean curd soup

Seafood

清炒大蝦 chīng-cháau daaih-hā
Stir-fried tiger prawns

清炒鮮魷 chīng-cháau sīn-yáu
Stir-fried squid

帶子炒蘆筍 daai-jí cháau lòh-sún
Stir-fried scallops with asparagus

燉鮑魚 dahn-bāau-yùeh Braised abalone

番茄小鮑魚煲 fāan-kàh síu-bāau-yùeh bō
Hot-pot of stewed abalone with tomato

薑葱炒龍蝦 gēung chūng cháau lùhng-ha
Stir-fried lobster with ginger and spring onions

薑葱清蒸三文魚 gēung chūng chīng-jīng
sāam-màhn-yùh
Steamed salmon with ginger and spring onions

姜葱蒸帶子 gēung chūng jīng daai-jí
Steamed scallops with ginger and spring onions

薑葱清蒸鰱魚 gēung chūng jīng lìhn-yùeh
Steamed chub with ginger and spring onions

姜葱蒸鱸魚 gēung chūng jīng lùh-yùh
Steamed sea bass with ginger and spring onions

海鮮粉絲煲 hói-sín fán-sī bō
Hot-pot of mixed seafood with vermicelli

紅燒鯉魚 hùhng-sīu léih-yùeh
Stewed carp with soya sauce, ginger and Chinese
wine

女兒紅酒蒸螃蟹 núih-yìh-hùhng-jáu jīng
pòhng-háaih
Steamed crab with Chinese rice wine

豉汁蒸鱔魚 sih-jāp jīng sihn-yùeh
Steamed eel with black bean sauce

豉汁蒸鮮魷 sih-jāp jīng sīn-yàuh
Steamed squid with black bean sauce

Poultry

白切雞 baahk-chit-gāi Boiled chicken

雞塊炒蘑菇 gāi-faai cháau mòh-gū
Stir-fried diced chicken with mushrooms

雞片炒蘆筍 gāi-pin cháau lòh-sún
Stir-fried shredded chicken with asparagus

姜葱炒雞塊 gēung chūng chao gāi-faai
Stir-fried diced chicken with ginger and spring
onions

烤雞 háau-gāi Roast chicken

紅燒雞 hùnhg-sīu-gāi Stewed diced chicken
with soya sauce and ginger

辣子炒雞丁 laahp-jí cháau gāi-dīng
Stir-fried diced chicken with chilli

栗子燉雞 luht-jí danh gāi
Braised chicken with chestnuts

腰果炒雞丁 yīu-gwóh cháau gāi-dīng
Stir-fried diced chicken with cashew nuts

Beef

姜葱炒牛肉 géung chūng cháau ngàuh-yuhk
Stir-fried beef with ginger and spring onions

紅燒牛肉 hùhng-sīu ngàuh-yuhk
Stewed beef with soya sauce and ginger

辣子牛肉煲 laahp-jí ngàuh-yuhk bō
Hot-pot diced beef with chilli

牛肉炒菠蘿 ngàuh-yuhk cháau bōh-lòhh
Stir-fried beef with pineapple

豉汁辣椒炒牛肉 sih-jāp laht-jīu chaau ngàuh-yuhk
Stir-fried beef with black bean sauce and chilli

薯仔燉牛肉 sùeh-jái dahn ngàuh-yuhk
Braised beef with potato

Duck, pork and lamb

叉燒 chā-sīu Roast pork

串燒羊肉塊 chuen-sīu yèunhg-yuhk-faai
Diced lamb kebab

燉羊肉 dahn yèuhng-yuhk
  Braised diced lamb with soya sauce and ginger

咕嚕肉 gū-lòh-yuhk Sweet and sour pork

烤鴨 hāau-aap Roast duck

椒盐排骨 jīu-yìhm pàaih-gwāt Roast pork
  spare ribs with pepper powder and salt

辣子炒肉丁 laht-jí cháau yuhk-dīng
  Stir-fried diced pork with chilli

辣椒炒鴨片 laht-jīu cháau aap-pin
  Stir-fried shredded duck with chilli

辣羊肉絲炒胡蘿蔔片 laht yèuhng-yuhk-sī
  cháau wòoh-lòhh-baahk-pin Stir-fried
  shredded lamb with sliced carrots and chilli

辣椒炒羊肉 laht-jīu cháau yèuhn-yuhk
  Stir-fried chicken or lamb with chilli and ginger

香酥鴨 sēung-sō-aap Crispy duck

豉汁蒸排骨 sih-jāp jīng pàaih-gwāt
  Steamed pork spare ribs with black bean sauce

酸梅汁蒸鴨塊 sūen-mòoih-jāp jīng-aap-faai
  Stewed diced duck with prune sauce

酸甜排骨 sūen-tìhm pàaih-gwāt
Sweet and sour pork spare ribs

羊肉煲 yèuhng-yuhk bō Lamb hot-pot

魚香肉片 yùeh-sēung yuhk-pin
Stir-fried shredded pork with fungus and chilli

肉片炒蘆筍 yuhk-pin cháau lòh-sún
Stir-fried shredded pork with asparagus

肉片炒黃瓜 yuhk-pin cháau wòhng-gwā
Stir-fried shredded pork with cucumber

肉絲炒青椒 yuhk-sī cháau chīng-jīu
Stir-fried shredded pork with green pepper

Vegetable and tofu/bean curd

蝦仁釀豆腐 hā-yàhn yeuhng dauh-fóo
Prawn stuffed tofu/beancurd

蠔油炒菜心 hòh-yáu cháau choi-sām
Stir-fried Chinese greens with oyster sauce

蠔油炒蘆筍 hòh-yáu cháau lòh-sún
Stir-fried asparagus with oyster sauce

185

海鮮豆腐煲 hói-sín dauh-fóo bō
Hot-pot of tofu/bean curd and mixed seafood

紅燒素豆腐 hùhng-sīu so dauh-fuh
Braised tofu (without meat)

涼拌海帶絲 lèuhng-poon hói-daai-sī
Sliced seaweed marinated with soya sauce,
garlic, vinegar and sesame oil

涼拌黃瓜絲 lèuhng-poon wòhng-gwā-sī
Sliced cucumber marinated with soya sauce,
garlic, vinegar and sesame oil

素炒豆芽 so-cháau dauh-ngàh
Stir-fried bean sprouts

蒜蓉炒青椒 sūen-yùhng cháau chīng-jīu
Stir-fried green peppers with garlic

蒜蓉炒蘑菇 sūen-yùhng cháau mó-gū
Stir-fried mushrooms with garlic

蒜蓉炒大白菜 sūen-yúng cháau daaih-
baahk-choi Stir-fried Chinese leaf with garlic

蒜蓉蚝油炒青菜 suen-yùhng hòh-yàuh
cháau chēng-choi Stir-fried Chinese greens
with garlic and oyster sauce

釀豆腐 yeuhng dauh-fuh Stuffed tofu

肉末釀豆腐 yuhk-mòoht yeuhng dauh-fóo
Minced pork stuffed with tofu/bean curd

Rice, noodles and dumplings

飯 faahn Steamed rice

海鮮炒面 hói-sīn cháau mihn
Fried noodles with seafood

蛋炒飯 daahn cháau faahn Egg fried rice

海鮮湯麵 hói-sín tōng mihn
Noodle soup with mixed seafood

雜菜湯麵 jaahp-choi tōng mihn
Noodle soup with mixed vegetables

蒸饅頭 jīng màahn-tàuh Steamed bun

龍蝦炒麵 lùnhg-hā cháau mihn
Stir-fried lobster with noodles

素炒麵 so cháau mihn Fried noodles

羊肉餃子 yèuhng-yuhk gáau-jí
Minced lamb dumplings

雞蛋炒番茄 gāi-daahn cháau fān-kèh
Stir-fried eggs with tomato

雞蛋炒蝦 gāi-daahn cháau hā
Stir-fried eggs with peeled prawns

Grammar

Grammatically, Cantonese is very easy and straight-forward when compared to English and to other European languages.

Verbs do not have different tenses and thus do not change in the past tense or in the past participle. There are no regular and irregular verbs. The structure of a question is the same as that of a statement – simply adding an extra character 嗎 (mā) to the end of a sentence turns it into a question.

Cantonese does not have grammatical gender and words therefore do not have a masculine and a feminine form, unlike languages such as French and Italian (although certain Chinese words refer specifically to males or to females, like in English 'pretty' is used for females and 'handsome' for males).

There is no difference between the singular and plural forms of nouns.

189

Nouns

• •

A noun is a word such as 'car', 'horse' or 'Mary' which is used to refer to a person or thing.

Like in English, Cantonese nouns are unisex: they do not have a male or female gender.

Cantonese articles are: 這 (je) = this
那 (náh) = that

The English definite article 'the' does not exist in Cantonese.

一 (yāt) in Cantonese is equivalent to the English 'a', 'an' or 'one'.

Note: Unlike English, Cantonese nouns use 'measure words' which indicate the quantity of a given noun. For example, where in English 'one horse' is used, Cantonese uses 'one + measure word for horse + horse': 一匹馬 (yāt-pāt máh). There are different measure words for different nouns; the basic ones are as follows:

個 (go) is used most frequently, and can be used with things, people and with most nouns. Usage of this measure word is possible with all nouns if the proper measure word is unknown, as Chinese people will still understand you.

List of most used measure words:-

本 (bún) for book, notebook, dictionary and magazine only;

輛 (léung) for automobile, train, bicycle and motor bike only;

架 (ga) for aircraft;

匹 (pāt) for horse;

頭 (tàuh) for pig, cow, sheep, dog only;

尾 (mei) for fish;

艘 (sáu) for boat, ship;

隻 (jek) for poultry

191

Pronouns

••

A pronoun is a word that you use to refer to
someone or something when you do not need to
use a noun, often because the person or thing has
been mentioned earlier. Examples are 'it', 'she/he',
'something' and 'myself'.

They are easier in Cantonese than in English;
all pronouns in Cantonese stay the same whether
they are used as subjects or objects.

Subject	Object	Cantonese pronouns (for both subjects and objects)
I	me	我 (ngóh)
you (singular)	you	你 (néih)
you (plural)	you	你們 (néih-mùhn)
he	him	他 (tā)
she	her	她 (tā)
it (animals/ objects)	it	牠/它 (tā)
we	us	我們 (ngóh-mùhn)
they (animals/ objects)	them	他/她們 (tā-mùhn)
things	them	牠/它們 (tā-mùhn)

Adjectives

An adjective is a word such as 'small', 'pretty' or 'practical' that describes a person or thing, or gives extra information about them.

In Cantonese, adjectives go either before or after the noun they describe: 紅蘋果 (hùhng pìhng-gwó) (the red apple) or 蘋果是紅的 (pìhng-gwó sih hùhng-dīk) (the apple is red). Note that 是 (sih) (to be) and 的 (dīk) go before and after the adjective in the latter case.

In Cantonese, some adjectives are only used to describe men and others are only used to describe women:

英俊的小伙子 (yīng-jun-dīk síu-fó-jí)
(handsome young man)
and
漂亮的姑娘 (piu-leuhng-dīk gū-nèuhng)
(pretty girl)

Possessives

. . . .

My, your, his, her, our, their

In Cantonese, you simply add 的 (dīk) to the end of
the above pronouns to make them possessives:

my	我的	(ngóh–dīk)
your (singular)	你的	(néih–dīk)
you (plural)	你們的	(néih–mùhn–dīk)
his	他的	(tā–dīk)
her	她的	(tā–dīk)
its (animals/ objects)	牠/它的	(tā–dīk)
our	我們的	(ngóh–mùhn–dīk)
their	他/她們的	(tā–mùhn–dīk)
their (animals/ objects)	牠們/它們的	(tā–mùhn–dīk)

Verbs

A verb is a word such as 'sing', 'walk' or 'cry' which is used with a subject to say what someone or something does or what happens to them.

Cantonese verbs are not divided into regular and irregular verbs, thus facilitating the construction of simple sentences:

我喜歡你 (ngóh héi-fūn néih) 'I like you'

In Cantonese, verbs do not have different tenses, such as past tense, present participle or past participle. Tenses are indicated through phrases such as 'yesterday' or 'in the past' which are placed before the verb and indicate, as in this case, that something happened or has happened. Another way of indicating the past is by adding 了 (líuh) after a verb that is being used to indicate the past tense:

我昨天去了倫敦 (ngóh johk-tīn heui-líuh lùhn-dūn) 'I went to London yesterday'

Note that Cantonese uses 'I yesterday go to London'.

When using a verb to indicate the present or past participle, you normally add 過 (gwo) after the verb:

我去過倫敦 (ngóh heui-gwo lùhn-dūn)
'I have/had been to London'.

List of most used verbs

吃	(sik) eat
買	(máaih) buy
賣	(maaih) sell
愛	(oi) love
去	(heui) go
喜歡	(héi-fūn) like

To form a negative, 不 (ngh) is placed before the verb: 我不吃 (ngóh-ngh-sīk) 'I am not eating'.

Building basic sentences

Like English, the structure of basic Chinese sentences is as follows:

I am Chinese	我是中國人	ngóh sih jūng-gwok-yàhn
I like you	我喜歡你	ngóh héi-fūn néih
Do you like me?	你喜歡我嗎?	néih héi-fūn ngóh mā?
I have been to Beijing	我去過北京	ngóh heui-gwok bāk-gīng

Grammar

Public holidays

· ·

National Holidays in Hong Kong

On national holidays you may find information offices closed, museums open for shorter hours and public transport running a limited service.

Note that Easter Monday changes every year, while all the other holidays keep to the same date.

1 January	New Year's Day (sān-nìhn)
	Chinese New Year *
	(jūng-gwok sān-nìhn)
	Easter Break (same as the UK)
	(fuhk-wuht ga-kèih)
1 October	National Day (gwok-hing-jit)
25 December	Christmas Day (sing-daan-jit)
26 December	Boxing Day (jit-láih-yaht)

* New Year (jūng-gwok sān-nìhn) falls on a different day on the western calendar (normally the first day of the Chinese New Year starts in late January to mid February) although it always starts

198

on the first day of the year on the Chinese lunar calendar.

Traditionally, families gather together, children receive money in 'red envelopes' and everyone helps make and eat a feast of chicken, fish etc. Families living in Northern China will have gáau jí 餃子, boiled dumplings with a thin skin, usually filled with pork and vegetables, as dinner on Chinese New Year's Eve. On greeting people over this festival it is traditional to wish them wealth and happiness, by saying gūng-héi faat-chòih 恭喜發財.

Yùhn-sīu-jit 元宵節 Yuensiu Festival, or Lantern Festival, is celebrated on the 15th day of the Lunar Chinese New Year. The traditional food which is eaten at this festival is also called yuensiu, or tōng-yùhn 湯圓, a traditional sweet dumpling made of glutinous rice, with various sweet fillings.

Dyūn-ńgh-jit 端午節, the Dragon Boat Festival, is celebrated on the 5th day of the 5th month of the Chinese lunar calendar. The two main activities which take place at this time are dragon boat racing and eating júng-jí 粽子, usually dates or meat

199

covered in sticky rice and wrapped in bamboo leaves. Both of these activities originate from the festival's traditional associations with the poet and statesman Qu Yuan. According to legend, Qu Yuan committed suicide by jumping into the Miluo River after his loyalty to the emperor was not rewarded. The story goes that local people took to their boats and threw jungji into the river to feed the fish, in the hope of rescuing his body.

Gwok–hing–jit 國慶節 National Day, on October 1st, commemorates the anniversary of the founding of the People's Republic of China, in 1949. The PRC was declared by Chairman Mao Zedong, in Tiananmen Square in Beijing.

Jūng–chāu–jit 中秋節 Mid-Autumn Festival, or Moon Festival, is celebrated on the 15th day of the 8th month of the Chinese lunar calendar. Traditionally, families gather to observe the moon and eat yueht–béng 月餅, mooncakes, which are round cakes made with a variety of sweet fillings including bean paste, egg and nuts etc. The roundness of both the full moon and the cakes symbolise the unity of the family.

Chīng-mìhng-jit 清明節 sometimes translated literally as Clear and Bright Festival, or Tomb Sweeping Festival, is celebrated on April 5th. It is traditionally the time when Chinese families visit graves to honour their dead ancestors and avoid eating hot food (the festival is sometimes also referred to as hòhn-sihk-jit 寒食節 or Cold Food Festival).

Signs and notices

When you are in Hong Kong either as a tourist or as a visitor, you will see Cantonese characters in airports, hotels, restaurants, parks and stations, and you will need to know their meaning in English.

General

入口	yahp-háu	entrance
出口	chūt-háu	exit
小心	síu-sām	caution
女厕	núih-chi	women's toilet
男厕	nàahm-chi	men's toilet
火警警報器	fó-gíng gíng-bo-hei	fire alarm

滅火器	miht-fó-hei	fire extinguisher
上	seuhng	up
下	hah	down
左	jó	left
右	yauh	right
止步	jí-bouh	keep out
失物認領	sāt-maht yihng-líhng	lost property
拉	lāi	pull
推	tēui	push
有人	yáu-yàhn	occupied
危險	ngàih-hím	danger
飲用水	yám-yuhng-séui	drinking water

非飲用水	fēi yám-yuhng-séui	non-drinking water
禁止入內	gam-jí yahp-noih	no entry
禁止吸煙	gam-jí kāp-yīn	no smoking
禁止游泳	gām-jí yàuh-wihng	no swimming
警報器	gíng-bo-hei	alarm

Airport/station

機場	gēi-chèuhng	airport
電梯	dihn-tāi	lift/elevator
地鐵站	deih-tit jaahm	underground station
火車站	fó-chē jaahm	train station
公共汽車站	gūng-guhng-hei-chē jaahm	bus station
行李認領	hàhng-léih yihn-líhng	baggage reclaim
免稅店	míhn-seui dim	duty free shops
開往	hōi-wóhng	bound for...
抵達	dái-daaht	arrivals
海關	hói-gwāan	customs

站檯	jaahm-tòih	platform
離境/發車	lèih-jihng/ faat-chē	departures
詢問處	sūn-mahn- chyu	information office
登機口	dāng-gēi-háu	boarding gate

Hotel/restaurant

衣帽室	yī-mó-sìh	cloakroom
冷水	láahng-séui	cold water
熱水	yiht-séui	hot water
接待處	jip-doih-chyu	reception
緊急出口	gán-gāp- chūt-háu	emergency/ fire exit

Shops

大減價	daaih-gáam-ga	sale
開門	hōi-mùhn	open
關門	gwāan-mùhn	closed
收款處	sāu-fún-chyu	cashier
電梯	dihn-tāi	lift

Sightseeing

兒童票	yìh-tùhng piu	child's ticket
成人票	sìhng-yàhn piu	adult ticket
學生票	hohk-sāang piu	student ticket

免費進入	míhn-fai jeun-yahp	free entry
請勿觸摸	chíng-màht chūk-mó	please don't touch
請勿入內	chíng-màht yahp-noih	no entry
請保持安靜	chíng-bó-chìh ōn-jihng	please keep quiet
禁止拍照	gām-jí paak-jiu	no photographs

On the street

電話亭	dihn-wá-tìhng	phone box
銀行	ngàhn-hòhng	bank
郵局	yàuh-guhk	post office

商場	sēung-chèuhng	shop
出租車	chūt-jō-chē	taxi
餐館	chāan-gún	restaurant
旅館	léuih-gún	hotel
醫院	yī-yúen	hospital
學校	hohk-haauh	school
圖書館	tòh-syū-gún	library
博物館	bok-maht-gún	museum
警察局	gíng-chaat-guhk	police station

A

English	Cantonese	English	Cantonese
a(n)	yāt	alarm	gíng-bo-hei
able	hó-yíh	alcohol	jáu-luih
accelerator	gā-chūk-hei	allergic to	dui ...
to accept	jip-sauh	alternator	gwo-mähn
accident	sih-gu/		gāau-làuh-
	yi-ngoih		faat-dihn-gēi
accident & emergency department	gáp-chán-sāt	ambulance	gau-wuh-chē
		anaemia	pành-huet- jìng
accommo- dation	jyuh-chyu	anaesthetic	màh-jui-jài
		and	wòh
address	deih-jí	another	lihng-ngoih- dīk
adult	daaih-yàhn	antibiotic	kong-
afternoon	hah-ńgh		sāang-so
age	nìhn-lìhng	antihistamine	kong-jo-n-jài
air conditioning	hūng-tiùh	antiseptic	saat-kwún-jài
airplane	fēi-gēi	apple	pìhng-gwó
airport	gēi-chèuhng	apricots	hahng-jí

English	Cantonese	English	Cantonese
April	四月 sei–yueht	baker's	麵包店 mihn–bāau–dim
arm	手臂 sáu–bei	ballet	芭蕾舞 bā–lùih–móh
arrivals (plane, train)	抵達 dái–daaht	banana	香蕉 hēung–jīu
asparagus	芦笋 lòuh–séun	bank	銀行 ngàhn–hòhng
asthma	哮喘病 hāau–chúen–behng	banknote	紙幣 jí–baih
aubergine	茄子 kéh–jí	bar	酒吧 jáu–bā
August	八月 baat–yueht	bathroom	浴室 yueh–sih
Australia	澳大利亞 o–daaih–leih–a	battery (radio, etc)	電池 dihn–chìh
autumn	秋天 chāu–tin	beach	沙灘 sā–tāan
		beautiful	美麗的 máih–laih–dīk
B		bed	床 chòhng
baby	嬰兒/寶貝 ying–yìh/bó–bui	double bed	雙人床 sēung–yàhn–chòhng
bad	壞 waaih	single bed	單人床 dāan–yàhn–chòhng
bag	袋 doih	bedroom	卧室 ngoh–sih
baggage reclaim	領取行李 líhng–chéui–hàhng–léih	beer	啤酒 bē–jáu

English – Cantonese

English – Cantonese

behind	在後面	joih-hauh-mihn
bicycle	自行車	jih-hàhng-chē
big	大些	daaih
bigger	大些	daaih-sē
bill (hotel, restaurant)	帳單	jeung-dāan
billion	十亿	sahp-yīk
birthday	生日	sāang-yaht
happy birthday!	生日快樂!	sāang-yaht faai-lohk!
my birthday is on…	我的生日是…	ngóh-dīk sāang-yaht sih…
birthday card	生日賀卡	sāang-yaht hoh-kāat
birthday present	生日禮物	sāang-yaht lìh-maht
biscuits	餅乾	béng-gōn
a bit	一點	yāt-dím
bitter (taste)	苦	fóo
black	黑色	hāak-sīk
bleach	去污液	heui-wū-yihk
blood	血	hyut
blood pressure	血壓	hyut-aat
high/low blood pressure	高/低血壓	gōu/dāi-hyut-aat
blouse	女襯衫	núih-chan-sāam
blue (light)	藍色的	làahm-sīk-dīk
boarding gate	登機口	dāng-gēi-háu
body	身體	sān-tái
bonnet	發動機罩盖	faat-duhng-gēi-jaau-gaai
book	書	syū
bookshop	書店	syū-dim

English	Cantonese		
boots (long)	長靴子	chèuhng-hēu-jí	
(ankle)	短靴子	dúen-hēu-jí	
bottle	瓶	pìhng	
a bottle of wine	一瓶葡萄酒	yāt-pìhng pòh-tòh-jáu	
bowl	碗	wóon	
box office	售票處	sauh-piu-chyu	
boy (young child)	男孩	nàahm-hàaih	
boyfriend	男朋友	nàahm-pàhng-yáuh	
brakes	刹車閘	saat-chē jaahp	
brand (make)	品牌	bán-pàaih	
brandy	白蘭地	baahk-làahn-dei	
breakfast	早餐	jóu-chāan	
bread	麵包	mihn-bāau	
breathing difficulties	呼吸困難	fōo-kàph-kwan-nàanh	
bride	新娘	sān-nèuhng	
bridegroom	新郎	sān-lòhng	
briefcase	手提箱	sáu-tàih-sēung	
Britain	英國	yīng-gwok	
British	英國的	yīng-gwok-dīk	
broccoli	西蘭花	sāi-làahn-fā	
brochure	小冊子	siu-chaak-jí	
bronchitis	支氣管炎	jī-hei-góon-yìhm	
brother	兄弟	hīng-daih	
brown	啡色	fē-sīk	
bulb (lightbulb)	燈泡	dāng-paau	
bureau de change	兌換處	deui-wuhn-chyu	
burger	漢堡包	hon-bó-bāau	

English – Cantonese

burglar	盜竊犯	douh-sit-faahn
bus	公共汽車	gūng-guhng-hei-chē
bus station	公共汽車站	gūng-guhng-hei-chē-jaahm
bus stop	公共汽車站	gūng-guhng-hei-chē jaahm
bus ticket	公共汽車票	gūng-guhng-hei-chē piu
business	公務	gūng-mouh
business trip	公差	gūng-chāi
butcher's	肉店	yuhk-dim
butter	黃油	wòhn-yàuh
by (next to)	鄰近	lùhn-gahn

by bus	搭公共汽車	dāap gūng-guhng-hei-chē
by car	坐私家車	chóh sī-gā-chē
by train	坐火車	chóh fó-chē

C

cab (taxi)	出租車	chūt-jō-chē
café	咖啡吧	ga-fē-bā
cake	蛋糕	daahn-gōu
cake shop	蛋糕店	daahn-gōu-dim
call (phone call)	打 (電話)	dá (dihn-wá)
calligraphy	書法	sūe-faat
camcorder	錄影機	luhk-sèuhng-gēi
camera	相機	sèuhng-gēi
campsite	野營地	ye-ying-dei
can (to be able)	可以/能	hó-yíh/nàhng

English		
can I...?	我可以/能 ... 嗎?	ngóh hó-yíh/ nàhng ... mā?
can we...?	我們可以/能 ... 嗎?	ngóh-múhn hó-yíh/nàhng ... mā?
Canada	加拿大	gā-nàh-daaih
Cantonese (language)	廣東話	gwóng-dūng-wá
capital (city)	首都	sáu-dō
car	私家車	sī-gā-chē
carrots	紅蘿蔔	hùhng-lòh-baahk
cartoons	卡通片	kā-tūng-pin
cash	現金	yihn-gām
to cash (cheque)	兌現 (支票)	deui-yihn (jī-piu)
cash desk	現金櫃檯	yihn-gām gwaih-tòih
cash machine	取鈔機	chéui-chāau-gēi
cashier	收款處	sāu-fún-chyu
casualty department	急診部	gāp-chán-boh
cat	猫	māau
cauliflower	菜花	choi-fā
caution	小心	siu-sām
CD	光碟	gwōng-dihp
celery	芹菜	kàhn-choi
chair	椅子	yí-jí
to change (money)	換子 (錢)	wuhn (chìhn)
charge (fee)	收費	sāu-fai
to charge (mobile, etc)	充電	chūng-dihn
cheap	便宜的	pìhn-yìh-dīk

English – Cantonese

to check in (airport/hotel)	辦理登機/入住手續	baahn-léih-dāng-gēi/yahp-jyuh-sáu-juhk
cheers!	乾杯!	gōn-būi!
cheese	奶酪	náaih-lok
chemist's	藥店	yeuhk-dim
cheque	支票	jī-piu
cherries	櫻桃	yīng-tòh
chest	胸腔	hūng-hōng
chicken	雞	gāi
chicken breast	雞胸肉	gāi-hūng-yuhk
chilli	辣椒	laaht-jīu
child	孩子	hàaih-jí
children	孩子們	hàaih-jí-mùhn
china	中國	jūng-gwok
Chinese (language)	漢語	hon-yúh
Chinese (person)	中國人	jūng-gwok yàhn
Chinese green tea	中國綠茶	jūng-gwok luhk-chàh
Chinese tea	中國茶	jūng-gwok chàh
chips (french fries)	炸薯條	ja-syùh-tiuh
chocolate	朱古力	jyū-gū-lihk
choke	阻風門	jó-fūng-muhn
chopsticks	筷子	faai-jí
Merry Christmas!	聖誕節 聖誕快樂!	sing-daan-jit sing-daan-faai-lohk!
church	教堂	gaau-tòhng
cigarette	香煙	hēung-yīn
cigarette lighter	打火機	dá-fó-gēi
cinema	電影院	dihn-yíng-yún
city	城市	sìhng-síh

English	Cantonese		English	Cantonese
cloakroom	衣帽間	yī-moh-gāan	Coke®	可樂	hó-lohk
clock	鬧鐘	naauh-jūng	cold	冷的	láahng-dīk
clothes	衣服	yī-fuhk	cold water	冷水	láahng-séui
Cloisonné	景泰藍	gíng-taai-làahm	I have a cold	我感冒了	ngóh gám-moh-líuh
clothes	衣物店	yī-maht-dim	colleague	同事	tòhng-si
cloudy	多云	dōh-wàhn	come in!	請進!	chíng-jeun!
clutch	離合器	leih-hahp-hei	complaint	投訴	tàuh-sou
coach	長途客車	chèuhng-tòh-haak-chē	computer	電腦	dihn-nóuh
			concert	音樂會	yām-ngohk-wúi
coat	大衣	daaih-yī	condoms	避孕套	beih-yahn-tou
cocktail	雞尾酒	gāi-méih-jáu	conference	會議	wuih-yíh
coffee	咖啡	gā-fē	congratulations	祝賀/恭喜	jūk-hoh/gūng-héi
(instant)	速溶咖啡	chūk-yùhng-ga-fē			
black coffee	咖啡不加奶	gā-fē ngh gā náaih	contract	合同	hahp-tùhng
			copy (verb/ noun)	複印/複印件	fūk-yan/fūk-yan-gihn
white coffee	咖啡加奶	gā-fē gā náaih	corner (of road)	(路) 邊	(loh)-bīn
coin	硬幣	ngaahng-baih			

English – Cantonese

English – Cantonese

cosmetics	fa-jōng-bán	化裝品	December	sahp-yih-yueht	十二月
country (nation)	gwok-gā	國家	delay	yìhn-ngh	延誤
cream	náaih-yàuh	奶油	delay (on train noticeboards)	ngh-dím	誤點
credit card	sun-yuhng-kāat	信用卡			
crisps	syùh-pín	薯片	dentist	ngàh-yī	牙醫
crossroads	sahp-jih-louh-háu	十字路口	department store	baak-fo-sēung-dim	百貨商店
cucumber	wòhng-gwā	黃瓜	departure	héi-fēi	起飛
customs (duty)	hói-gwāan	海關	departures lounge	hauh-gēi-tēng	候機廳
D			deposit	dihng-gām	定金
danger	nàaih-hím	危險	dessert	tìhm-bán	甜品
date	yaht-kèih	日期	diabetes	tòhng-niuh-behng	糖尿病
date of birth	sāang-yaht	生日	diabetic	waahn-tòhng-niuh-behng	患糖尿病
daughter	núih-yìh	女兒			
daughter-in-law	yìh-sīk-fúh	兒媳婦			
dear	chàn-oi-dīk	親愛的			

English	Chinese	Cantonese
I'm diabetic	我是糖尿病患者	ngóh-sih-tòhng-niuh-behng-waahn-jé
dictionary	字典	jih-dín
diesel	柴油	chàaih-yàu
diet	節食	jit-sihk
digital camera	数码相機	sou-máh sēung-gēi
dining room	餐廳	chāan-tēng
dinner (evening meal)	晚餐	máahn-chāan
directions	方向	fōng-heuhng
directory (telephone)	電話簿	dihn-wá-bó
dirty	飢髒的	hòhng-jōng-dik
disabled (person)	殘疾人	chàahn-jaht-yàhn
discount	折扣	jit-kau
distributor (car)	分销商	fān-sīu-sēung
doctor	醫生	yī-sāang
documents	文件	màhn-gihn
dog	狗	gáu
domestic	國内的	gwok-noih-dik
door	門	mùhn
double	雙人	sēung-yàhn
double bed	雙人床	sēuhng-yàhn-chòhng
double room	雙人房	sēung-yàhn-fòhng
down	下	hah
down there	在那裏	joih nàh-léih
downstairs	摟下	làuh-hah
dress (soft)	連衣裙	lihn-yī-kwàhn
drink (soft)	飲料	yám-liuh
drinking water	飲用水	yám-yuhng-séui

English – Cantonese

English – Cantonese

English	Cantonese	Romanization
non-drinking water	非飲用水	fēi-yám-yuhng-séui
driver (of car)	司機	sī-gēi
driving licence	駕駛証	ga-sái-jing
drug (medicine)	藥	yeuhk
drug (narcotics)	毒品	duhk-bán
dry-cleaner's	乾洗店	gōn-sái-dim
duty-free	免稅	mihn-seui
duty free shops	免稅店	mihn-seui-dim
E		
earphones	耳機	yíh-gēi
Easter	復活節	fuk-wuht-jit
egg	蛋	dáan
eight	八	baat
eighteen	十八	sahp-baat
eighth	第八	daih-baat
eighty	八十	baat-sahp
electric point	電源	dihn-yùehn
electricity	電	dihn
eleven	十一	sahp-yāt
e-mail	電子郵件	dihn-jí-yàuh-gihn
embassy	大使館	daaih-si-gún
emergency	緊急事件	gán-gáp sih-gihn
emergency exit	緊急出口	gán-gáp chùt-háu
engine	發動機	faat-duhng-gēi
England	英格蘭	yīng-gaak-làahn
English (person)	英國人	yīng-gwok-yàhn
English (language)	英語	yīng-yúeh
entrance	入口	yahp-háu
entrance fee	入場費	yahp-chèuhng-fai

English		
equipment	設備	chit-beih
Europe	歐洲	āu-jāu
evening	晚上	māahn-seuhng
this evening	今晚	gām-máahn
tomorrow evening	明晚	mìhng-máahn
exchange rate	兌換率	deui-wuhn-luht
excuse me! (sorry)	對不起!	deui-ngh-jueh!
(when passing)	請讓一讓!	ching-yeuhng-yāt-yeuhng!
exhaust (car)	廢氣	fai-hei
exhibition	展覽	jín-áahm
exit	出口	chùt-háu
expensive	昂貴的	ngòhng-gwai-dik
eye	眼睛	ngáahn-jīng

F

face	臉	líhm
family	家庭	g-tìhng
far: is it far?	遠嗎?	yúehn-mā?
father	父親	fuh-chān
fax	傳真	chùehn-jān
February	二月	yih-yueht
feet	腳	geuk
female	女的	núih-dik
fever	發燒	faat-sìu
fiancé(e)	未婚夫妻	meih-fān-fūh/chāi
fifteen	十五	sahp-ńgh
fifth	第五	daih-ńgh
fifty	五十	ńgh-sahp
film (at cinema)	電影	dihn-yíng
fine	好	hó
fine, thanks	好, 謝謝	hó, jeh-jeh
finger	手指	sáu-jí

English - Cantonese

fire	火	fó
fire!	着火了！	jeuhk-fó-liuh!
fire alarm	火警報警器	fó-gíng bo-gíng-hei
fire brigade	消防隊	siu-fòhng-duih
fire escape	太平梯	taai-pìhng-tāi
fire extinguisher	滅火器	miht-fó-hei
firemen	消防員	siu-fòhng-yùhn
first	第一	daih-yāt
first aid	急救	gāp-gau
first class	一等艙／一等車廂	yāt-dáng-chōng／yāt-dáng-chē-sēung
fish	魚	yùh
five	五	ńgh

flight	航班	hòhng-bāan
flour	麵粉	mihn-fán
flowers	花	fā
flu	流感	làuh-gám
fog	霧	moh
food	食物	sihk-maht
food poisoning	食物中毒	sihk-maht-jùng-duhk
foot	脚	geuk
football	足球	jūk-kàuh
foreigner	外國人	ngoih-gwok-yàhn
fork (for eating)	叉	chā
fountain	噴泉	pan-chùehn
four	四	sei
fourteen	十四	sahp-sei
fourth	第四	daih-sei
forty	四十	sei-sahp
France	法國	faat-gwok

English		
free entry	免費進入	mihn-fai jeun-yahp
French (language)	法語	faat-yúh
French (person)	法國人	faat-gwok-yàhn
Friday	星期五	sīng-keih-ńgh
friend	朋友	pàhng-yáuh
fruit	水果	séui-gwó
fruit juice	果汁	gwó-jāp
fruit shop	水果店	séui-gwó-dim
fuse	保險絲	bó-hím-sī

G

gallery	美術館	méih-suht-gún
garage	修車行	sāu-chē-hòhng
garden	花園	fā-yùehn
garlic	大蒜	daaih-suen
gate (airport)	登機口	dāng-gēi-háu

gears	換檔	wuhn-dong
gents (toilet)	男廁所	nàahm-chi-só
German (language)	德語	dē-yúh
German (person)	德國人	dē-gwok-yàhn
Germany	德國	dē-gwok
gift	禮物	láih-maht
gift shop	禮品店	láih-bán-dim
girl	女孩	núih-hàaih
girlfriend	女朋友	núih-pàhng-yáuh
glass (substance)	玻璃	bō-lèih
glass (for drinking)	玻璃杯	bō-lèih-būi
a glass of water	一杯水	yāt būi séui
a glass of wine	一杯葡萄酒	yāt būi pòh-tòh-jáu
I'm going to...	我正要去…	ngóh jing-yiu-heui…

English – Cantonese

English – Cantonese

we're going to...	我們正要去…	ngóh-mùhn jing-yiu-heui...
good	好	hó
goodbye	再見	joi-gin
good evening	晚安	máahn-ōn
good night	晚安	máahn-ōn
gram	克	hàk
grapefruit	葡萄柚	pòh-tòh-yáu
grapes	葡萄	pòh-tòh
green (colour)	綠色	luhk-sik
green tea	綠茶	uhk-chàh
grey	灰色	fūi-sik
grocer's	雜貨店	jaahp-fo-dim
ground floor	一樓	yāt-láuh
guide (tourist)	導遊	doh-yàuh
guidebook	導遊冊	doh-yàuh-chaak

guided tour	有導遊的遊覽	yáuh-doh-yàuh-dīk yàuh-láahm
H		
hair	頭髮	tàuh-faat
hairdresser	美髮師	méih-faat-sī
hairdresser's	髮廊	faat-lòhng
half	一半	yāt-bun
half-price	半價	bun-ga
hamburger	漢堡包	hon-bó-bāau
hand	手	sáu
handbag	手提包	sáu-tàih-bāau
handbrake	手剎	sáu-saat
handicapped	有殘疾的	yáuh-chàahn-jaht-dīk
hand luggage	手提行李	sáu-tàih hàhng-léih
happy	快樂	faai-lohk

English	Chinese	Romanization	English	Chinese	Romanization
happy Anniversary!	紀念日快樂!	géi-neihm-yaht faai-lohk!	heart disease	心臟病	sàm-johng-behng
Happy birthday!	生日快樂!	sàang-yaht-faai-lohk!	heating	暖氣	nuehn-hei
happy Easter!	復活節快樂!	fuhk-wuht-jit faai-lohk!	hello!	你好!	néih-hó!
happy New Year!	新年快樂!	sàn-nìhn faai-lohk!	help!	救命啊!	gau-mehng-à!
I have...	我有...	ngóh-yáuh...	to help	幫助	bòng-joh
we have...	我們有...	ngóh-mùhn-yáuh...	can you help me?	你能幫助我嗎?	néih-nàhng-bòng-joh-ngóh mà?
have a good trip!	一路順風!	yāt-loh suhn-fùng!	her	她的	tā-dīk
he	他	tā	here is...	這裏是...	je-léih-sih...
head	頭	tàuh	here is my passport	這是我的護照	je-sih ngóh-dīk wuh-jiu
headache	頭痛	tàuh-tung	him	他	tā
headlights	車頭燈	chē-tàu-dāng	car hire	租借車	jō-je-chē
heart	心	sàm	his	他的	tā-dīk
heart beat	心跳	sàm-tiu	holiday	度假	doh-gá
			home	家	gā
			hospital	醫院	yì-yúen

English – Cantonese

hot	熱	yiht
hot water	熱水	yiht-séui
hotel	旅館	léuih-gún
how are you?	你好嗎?	néih-hó-mā?
how do I get...?	我怎麼...?	ngóh jám-móh...?
how much is it?	多少錢?	dō-síu-chìhn?
hundred	一百	yāt-baak
hungry	餓	ngoh
I	我	ngóh
ice	冰	bīng
ice-cream	冰淇淋	bīng-kèih-làhm
ice-lolly	冰條	bīng-tiùh
identity card	身份証	sān-fahn-jing
ignition	點火	dím-fó

ill	生病	sāang-behng
I'm ill	我病了	ngóh behng-liuh
indicator	顯示器	hín-sih-hei
infection	炎症	yìhm-jing
information	資訊	jī-sun
insurance	保險	bó-hím
fully comprehensive insurance	全保險	chùehn-bó-him
international	國際的	gwok-jaih-dīk
invitation	邀請	yāo-chíng
Ireland	愛爾蘭	oi-yíh-làahn
iron (for clothes)	熨斗	tong-dáu
island	島	dó
Italian (language)	意大利語	yi-daaih-leih yúh
Italian (person)	意大利人	yi-daaih-leih yàhn

English	Cantonese		English	Cantonese
Italy	意大利	yi-daaih-leih			
			keep out	止步	ji-bouh
J			key	鎖匙	sóh-sih
jacket	短上衣	dúen-seuhng-yī	kilogram	公斤	gūng-gān
			kilometre	公里	gūng-léih
jade	玉石	yueh-sehk	kind (person)	友善的	yáuh-sihn-dīk
jam (food)	果醬	gwóh-jeung	kiosk	收銀處	sāu-ngàhn-chyu
January	一月	yāt-yueht			
jeweller's	珠寶店	jyū-bóu-dim	knickers	女內褲	núih-dái-fu
jewellery	珠寶	jyū-bó	to knock (on door)	敲(門)	hāau (mùhn)
Jewish	猶太人	yàu-taai yàhn	to know (facts)	知道	ji-dou
job	工作	gūng-jok	I don't know	我不知道	ngóh-ngh-ji-dou
to joke	開玩笑	hōi-wáahn-siu			
journalist	記者	gei-jé			
journey	旅程	léuih-chìhng	**L**		
July	七月	chāt-yueht	ladies (toilet)	女廁所	núih-chi-so
jumper	毛衣	làahm-sāam	lady	女仕	núih-sih
June	六月	luhk-yueht	lamp	台燈燈	tòih-dāng

English – Cantonese

language	語言	yùh-yìhn	*I like coffee*	我喜歡咖啡	ngóh héi-fūn gā-fē
large	大	daaih	*I don't like...*	我不喜歡...	ngóh ngh héi-fūn...
left (not right)	左	jó			
left-luggage	行李寄存	hàhng-léih gei-chyùhn	*liqueur*	烈酒	liht-jáu
leg	腿	téui	*litre*	升	sing
lemon	檸檬	nìhng-mūng	*a little...*	一點...	yāt-dím...
lemonade	七喜	chāt-héi	*I live in...*	住在...	jyuh-joih...
less	更小的	gàang-siu-dīk	*I live in London*	我住在倫敦	ngóh jyuh-joih lùhn-dūn...
letter	信	sun			
library	圖書館	tòh-syū-gún			
licence:			*long*	長的	chèuhng-dīk
driving licence	駕駛証	ga-sái-jìhng	*to lose*	丟失	diu-sāt
lift (elevator)	電梯	dihn-tāi	*I've lost my...*	我丟失了我的...	ngóh diu-sāt-liuh ngóh-dīk...
like	喜歡	héih-fūn			
I'd like...	我想...	ngóh-séung...	*lost property*	失物認領	sāt-maht yihng-líhng
we'd like...	我們想...	ngóh-mùhn séung...			

English		
lost property office	失物認領處	sāt-maht yihng-lihng-chyu
love	愛	oi
luggage	行李	hàhng-léih
luggage trolley	行李手推車	hàhng-léih-sáu-tēui-chē
lunch	午飯	ńgh-faahn

M

Madam/Ms...	女仕	néuih-sih
magazine	雜誌	jaahp-ji
male	男人	nàahm-dīk
man	男人	nàahm-yàhn
manager	經理	gīng-léih
Mandarin (language)	普通話	póu-tūng-wá
map (of country)	地圖	deih-tòuh
March	三月	sāam-yueht
married	结婚了	git-fān-liuh
I'm married	我已經结婚了	ngóh yi-gīng git-fān-liuh
are you married?	你结婚了嗎?	néih git-fān-liuh-liuh-mā?
May	五月	ńgh-yueht
meal	飯	faahn
meat	肉	yuhk
medicine	藥	yeuhk
meet	會面	wuih-mihn
pleased to meet you!	革命!	hahng-wuih-wuih!
melon	瓜	gwā
menu	菜單	choi-dāan
message	留言	làuh-yìhn
metro (underground)	地鐵	deih-tit
metro station	地鐵站	deih-tit-jaahm
military police	軍警	gwān-gíng

English – Cantonese

English	Cantonese		English	Cantonese	
milk	牛奶	ngàuh-nàaih	money	錢	chihn
million	一百萬	yāt-baak-maahn	I have no money	我沒有錢	ngóh moh-chihn
mind: do you mind?	你介意嗎?	néih gaai-yi mà?	month	月	yueht
I don't mind	我不介意	ngóh ngh gaai-yi	monthly	每月	múih-yueht
mineral water	礦泉水	kwong-chuehn-séui	more	更多的	gāang-dō-dik
			morning	早晨	jó-sàhn
Ming porcelain	明瓷器	mihng-chih-hei	mother	母親	móh-chān
minute	分鐘	fàn-jūng	motorway	高速公路	gō-chūk-gūng-louh
to miss (train, etc)	誤了	ngh-liuh	mouth	嘴	jéui
			movie	電影	dihn-yíng
Miss...	...小姐	síu-jé	Mr.../Sir	...先生	sìn-sàang
mistake	錯誤	cho-ngh	Mrs...	...太太	taai-taai
mobile phone	手機	sáu-gēi	Ms.../Madam	女仕	néuih-sih
mobile number	手機號碼	sáu-gēi-hoh-máh	mugging	搶劫	chéung-gip
			museum	博物館	bok-maht-gún
Monday	星期一	sing-kèih-yāt	mushroom	蘑菇	mòh-gū
			music	音樂	yām-ngohk

musical production	歌劇	gōh-kehk
my	我的	ngóh-dīk
N		
name	名字	mihng-jih
my name is...	我的名字是...	ngóh-dīk mihng-jih-sih...
what is your name?	你叫甚麼名字?	néih giu sahm-mō mihng-jih?
nationality	國籍	gwok-jihk
near to...	靠近...	kaoh-gahn...
need: I need...	我需要...	ngóh sēui-yiu...
we need...	我們需要...	ngóh-mùhn sēui-yiu...
new	新的	sān-dīk
news	新聞	sān-màhn

newsagent	報攤	bo-tāan
newspaper	報紙	bou-jí
New Year	新年	sān-nìhn
Happy New Year!	新年快樂!	sān-nìhn-faai-lohk!
New Zealand	新西蘭	sān-sāi-làahn
next to	旁邊的	póhng-bīn-dīk
nine	九	gáu
nineteen	十九	sahp-gáu
ninety	九十	gáu-sahp
ninth	第九	daih-gáu
no	不	ngh
no, thanks	不用, 多謝	ngh, sái, (dō)-jeh
no entry	請勿入內	chíng-maht yahp-noih
non smoking	禁煙區	gám-yīn-kēui
no smoking	不準抽煙	ngh-jún-chāu-yīn

English – Cantonese

English – Cantonese

English	Cantonese	Romanization
no swimming	禁止游泳	gàm-jí-yàuh-wìhng
noise	噪音	chou-yàm
Northern Ireland	北愛爾蘭	bāk-oi-yíh-làahn
nose	鼻子	beih-jí
not	不	ngh
I do not know	我不知道	ngóh-ngh-jì-doh
novel	小說	síu-suet
number	號碼	hoh-máh
O		
oats	麥片	màkh-pin
October	十月	sahp-yueht
office	辦公室	baahn-gūng-sih
ticket office	售票處	sauh-piu-chyu
OK!	好!	hóu!
old (not young)	老 (不年輕)	lóuh (bāt-nìhn-hìng)
old: how old are you?	你多大年紀了?	néih dō daaih nìhn-jéi-líuh?
I'm ... years old	我 ... 歲了	ngóh ... seui-líuh
olive oil	橄欖油	gàm-láahm-yàuh
at once	馬上	ma-séuhng
one	一	yāt
onion	洋葱	yèuhng-chùng
open	打開	dá-hòi
when does it open?	郵局基麼時間開門?	yàuh-gúk sahm-mó sih-gāan hòi-mùhn?
opium pipe	鴉片煙斗	ā-pin-yìn-dáu
opposite	對面的	dui-mihn dìk

optician	眼镜商	ngáahn-geng-sēung	painting (picture)	畫	wá
orange (colour)	橙色	cháang-sīk	pair	雙/對	sēung/deui
orange (fruit)	橙子	cháang-jí	palace	宮殿	gūng-dihn
orange juice	橙汁	cháang-jāp	paper	紙	jí
freshly squeezed orange juice	鲜榨橙汁	sīn-ja cháang-jāp	pardon?	你說甚麼?	néih suet sahm-mō?
our	我們的	ngóh-mùhn-dīk	I beg your pardon?	請你再說一遍?	chíng néih joi suet-yāt-pin?
owe	我欠你…	ngóh him néih...	parents	父母	fuh-móuh
I owe you...		néih him...	park	公園	gūng-yúehn
you owe me...	你欠我…	ngóh...	to park	停車	tìhng-chē
			partner (business)	合伙人	hahp-fó-yàhn
P			partner (boy/girlfriend)	伴侣	boohn-lúih
package	包裹	bāau-gwó	party (celebration)	晚會	máahn-wuih
pain	痛	tung	passenger	旅客	lúih-haak

English – Cantonese

English – Cantonese

passport	護照	wuh-jiu
to pay	支付	jí-fuh
I want to pay	我想付款	ngóh séung fuh-fún
where do I pay?	我在哪裏付款？	ngóh joih náh-léih fuh-fún?
payment	付款	fuh-fún
peaches	桃子	tòh-jí
peanut allergy	對花生過敏	deui fā-sāang gwoh-máhn
pears	梨	lèih
peas	豌豆	wún-dauh
pen	筆	bit
people	人們	yàhn-mùhn
pepper (spice)	胡椒	wùh-jiu
pepper (vegetable)	青椒	chēng-jiu
perfume shop	香水店	hēung-séui-dim

person	人	yàhn
petrol	汽油	hei-yàuh
petrol station	加油站	gā-yàu-jaahm
pharmacy	藥店	yeuhk-dim
phone	電話	dihn-wá
phone box	電話亭	dihn-wá-tìhng
phonecard	電話卡	dihn-wá-kāat
photograph	相片	sèuhng-pin
photographic shop	相館	seung-góon
phrasebook	短語集	dúen-yúh-jaahp
pillow	枕頭	jám-tàuh
pink	粉紅色	fán-hùhng-sik
pity: what a pity!	真可惜！	jān-hó-sik!
place	地方	deih-fōng
place of birth	出生地	chùt-sāang-deih

English	Cantonese (characters)	Romanization
plane	飛機	fēi-gēi
plate	碟子	dihp-jí
platform (railway)	站檯	jaahm-tòih
play (theatre)	演出	yín-chūt
please	請	chíng
pleased to meet you	認識你很高興	yihng-sīk-néih hán-gō-hing
plums	梨子	léih-jí
poisonous	有毒的	yáuh-duhk-dīk
police	警察	ging-chaat
military police	軍警	gwān-ging
police station	警察局	ging-chaat-guhk
pool (swimming)	游泳池	yàuh-wihng-chìh
pork	猪肉	jyū-yuhk
porter (for luggage)	行李搬運工	hàhng-léih-būn-wahn-gūng
Portugal	葡萄牙	pòh-tòh-ngàh
Portuguese (language)	葡萄牙語	pòh-tòh-ngàh-yúh
Portuguese (people)	葡萄牙人	pòh-tòh-ngàh-yàhn
postbox	郵箱	yàuh-sēung
postcard	明信片	mihng-sun-pin
postcode	郵政編碼	yàuh-jing-pín-máh
post office	郵政局	yàuh-jing-guhk
potato	薯仔	syùh-jái
present (gift)	禮物	láih-maht
price	價格	ga-gaak
private facilities	私人設施	sī-yàhn-chit-sī

English – Cantonese

problem	問題	mahn-tàih
to pronounce	發音	faat-yām
public holiday	公共假期	gūng-guhng-ga-kèih
to pull	拉	lāi
purse	錢包	chìhn-bāau
to push	推	tēui
pyjamas	睡衣	seuih-yī

Q

quality	質量	jāt-leuhng
quantity	數量	so-leuhng
to quarrel	爭吵	jāng-cháau
queue	排隊	pàaih-déui
quickly	快點	faai-dím
quiet (place)	安靜	ōn-jihng

R

| race (sport) | 賽跑 | choi-páau |

racket (tennis, etc)	球拍	kàuh-paak
radiator	散熱器	sáan-yiht-hei
radio	收音機	sāu-yām-gēi
railway station	火車站	fó-chē jaahm
rain	雨	yúh
to rain	落雨	lohk-yúh
raincoat	雨衣	yúh-yī
raped	被強姦	beih-kèuhng-gāan

rate of exchange	兌換率	deui-wuhn-leuht
receipt	收據	sāu-geui
reception (desk)	接待處	jip-doih-chyu
receptionist	接待員	jip-doih-yuehn
red	紅色的	hùhng-sīk-dīk
red wine	紅葡萄酒	hùhng pòh-tòh-jáu

| reduction | 減價 | gáam-ga |

English		Cantonese
refund	退款	teui-fún
register	註冊	jyu-chaak
registration form	註冊表格	jyu-chaak-biu-gaak
remote control	遙控	yìuh-hung
repair	修理	sāu-léih
to reserve	預定	yuh-dihng
to rest	休息	yāu-sīk
restaurant	餐館	chāan gún
retired: *I'm retired*	我退休了	ngóh teui-yāu-liúh
return ticket	往返票	wóhng-fáan-piu
reverse gear	後換檔	hauh-wuhn-dong
rice	米	máih
right (not left)	右	yauh
road	公路	gūng-louh
road map	公路地圖	gūng-louh-deih-tòh
road sign	路標	louh-bīu
room (hotel)	客房	haak-fòhng
double room	雙人房	sēung-yàhn-fòhng
single room	單人房	dāan-yàhn-fòhng
rose	玫瑰	mùih-gwai
rubbish	垃圾	laahp-saap

S

safe (for valuables)	保險櫃	bó-hím-gwaih
safe (medicine, etc)	安全的	ōn-chùehn-dīk
safety	安全	ōn-chùehn
salad	涼拌生菜	lèuhng-bun sāang-choi
sale	廉售	lìhm-sauh

English – Cantonese

salesman/ woman	销售員	síu-sauh-yuehn yihm	seatbelt	安全帶	ōn-chuehn-daai
salt	盐		second	第二	daih-yih
sand	沙	sā	second class	二等	yih-dáng
sandwich	三文治	sāam-mahn-jih	to see	看	tai
satellite TV	衛星電視	waih-sīng dihn-sih	see you later	過一陣見	gwoh-yāt-jahn-gin
Saturday	星期六	sīng-keih-luhk	see you		
school	學校	hohk-haauh	tomorrow	明天見	ming-tīn-gin
Scotland	蘇格蘭	sō-gaak-làahn	to sell	賣	maaih
Scottish	蘇格蘭人	sō-gaak-làahn yàhn	do you sell ...?	你們賣 ... 嗎?	néih-mùhn-maaih ... mà?
sea	大海	daaih-hói	September	九月	gáu-yueht
seafood	海鲜	hói-sīn	series/soap (TV)	連續劇	lìhn-juhk-kehk
seaside: at the seaside	在海邊	joih-hói-bīn	service charge	服务费	fuhk-moh-fai
season (of year)	季節	gwai-jit	set menu	套餐菜單	to-chāan-choi-dāan
seat (chair)	座位	joh-wái	seven	七	chāt
			seventeen	十七	sahp-chāt

English		Cantonese
seventh	第七	daih-chāt
seventy	七十	chāt-sahp
she	她	tā
sheet (bed)	床單	chòhng-dāan
shirt	襯衫	chan-sāam
shoe	鞋	hàaih
shoe shop	鞋店	hàaih-dim
shop	商店	sēung-dim
shorts	短褲	dúen-fu
shoulder	肩膀	gin-pòhng
sightseeing tour	觀光游覽	gūn-gwōng-yàuh-láahm
signature	簽名	chīm-mìhng
silk	絲綢	sī-chàuh
silk dress	真絲連衣裙	jān-sī-lìhn-yī-kwàhn
silk scarf	絲巾	sī-gān
silk tie	真絲領帶	jān-sī-lìhng-daai
silver	銀	ngàhn
single (unmarried)	單身的	dāan-sān-dīk
single bed	單人床	dāan-yàhn-chòhng
single room	單人房	dāan-yàhn-fòhng
single ticket	單程	dāan-chìhng
Sir	先生	sīn-sāang
sister	姐妹	jé-muih
to sit	坐下	chóh-dāi
please, sit down	請坐下	chíng-chóh-dāi
six	六	luhk
sixteen	十六	sahp-luhk
sixth	第六	daih-luhk
sixty	六十	luhk-sahp
skis	雪橇	suet-hīu
skin	皮膚	pèih-fū

English – Cantonese

English	Cantonese	Cantonese romanization
skirt	短裙	dúen-kwàhn
sky	天	tìn
to sleep	睡覺	seuih-gaau
small	小些	síu
smaller	小些	síu-sē
smoke: to smoke/smoking	抽煙	chàu-yìn
I don't smoke	我不抽煙	ngóh-ngh-chàu-yìn
can I smoke?	我可以抽煙嗎?	ngóh-hó-yíh-chàu-yìn-mà?
snow	雪	suet
to snow: it's snowing	正在落雪	jing-joih-lohk-suet
soap	肥皂	feìh-joh
soap powder	洗衣粉	sái-yì-fán
socks	短襪	dúen-maht
sofa	沙發	sà-faat

English	Cantonese	Cantonese romanization
soya sauce	生抽	sàang-chàu
soft drink	汽水	hei-séui
some more...	更多的	gang-dò-dìk
son	兒子	yìh-jí
song	歌	gò
sore throat	喉嚨痛	hàuh-lùhng-tung
sorry: I'm sorry!	對不起!	deui-ngh-jyuh!
soup	湯	tòng
souvenir	禮品	láih-bán
Spain	西班牙	sài-bàan-ngàh
Spanish (language)	西班牙語	sài-bàan-ngàh yúh
(people)	西班牙人	sài-bàan-ngàh yàhn
spark plug	火花塞	fó-fà-sàk
to speak	說	suet

English	Cantonese		English	Cantonese	
do you speak English?	你會說英文嗎?	néih sīk góng yīng-màhn mā?	stalls	正廳前排	jing-tēng-chihn-pàaih
I don't speak Mandarin	我不識說國語	ngóh-ngh-sīk-góng-gwok-yúeh	stamp	郵票	yàuh-piu
			start	開始	hōi-chí
speed limit	速度限制	chūk-douh haahn-jai	starter (food)	頭盤	tàuh-pùhn
speeding	超速	chīu-chūk	station	車站	chē-jaahm
spinach	波菜	bō-choi	to stay (remain)	住	jyuh
spirits (alcohol)	酒	jáu	I'm staying at…	我住在…	ngóh jyuh… joih…
spoon	起糞	chìh-gāng	to steal	偷	tāu
sports shop	體育用品商店	tái-yuhk yuhng-bán sēung-dim	steering	軚向	jūen-heung
			steering wheel	方向盤	fōng-heung-pòohn
spring (season)	春天	chūn-tīn	stomach	胃	waih
square (in town)	廣場	gwóng-chèuhng	stomachache	胃痛	waih-tung
			stone	石頭	sik-tàuh
staff	員工	yuehn-gūng	to stop (come to a halt)	停止	tihng-jí
			store	商場	sēung-chèuhng

English – Cantonese

English – Cantonese

English	Cantonese	Romanization	English	Cantonese	Romanization
straight on	一直往前走	yāt-jihk wòhng-chìhm-jáu	sunglasses	太陽鏡	taai-yèuhng-geng
strawberries	草莓	chó-mùih	supermarket	超市	chìu-síh
street	街道	gāai-douh	supper (dinner)	晚餐	máahn-chāan
street map	街道地圖	gāai-douh-deih-tòh	surname	姓	sing
			my surname is…	我姓…	ngóh sing…
student	學生	hohk-sāang	swimming pool	游泳池	yàuh-wihng-chìh
sugar	糖	tòhng	swimsuit	游泳衣	yàuh-wihng-yī
suit	西裝	sāi-jōng	Swiss (language)	瑞士語	seuih-sih yúh
suitcase	手提箱	shao-tàih-sēung	Swiss (people)	瑞士人	seuih-sih yàhn
summer	夏天	hah-tīn	to switch off	關	gwāan
sun	太陽	taai-yèuhng	to switch on	開	hōi
to sunbathe	日光浴	yaht-gwōng-yuhk	Switzerland	瑞士	seuih-sih
sunblock	防曬油	fòhng-saai-yàuh	**T**		
			table	檯	tòih
Sunday	星期日	sing-kèih-yáht	tablet (pill)	藥丸	yeuhk-yúehn

English	Cantonese	Pronunciation
table tennis	網球	móhng-kàuh
Tang poetry	唐詩	tòhng-sī
taxi	出租車	chūt-jō-chē
tea	茶	chàh
teacher	老師	lóuh-sī
teeth	牙	ngàh
telephone	電話	dihn-wá
to telephone	打電話	dá dihn-wá
telephone box	電話亭	dihn-wá-tìhng
telephone card	電話卡	dihn-wá-kāat
telephone number	電話號碼	dihn-wá houh-máh
television	電視	dihn-si
to tell	告訴	go-so
temperature	溫度	wàn-douh
to have a temperature	發燒	faat-sīu
ten	十	sahp
tennis	網球	móhng-kàuh
tenth	第十	daih-sahp
terracotta	兵馬俑	bīng-má-yúng
thank you	謝謝你	jeh-jeh-néih
thanks very much	多謝	dō-jeh
theatre	劇院	kehk-yuen
their	他們的	tā-mùhn-diik
there (over there)	那裏	náh-léih
there is/ there are	有	yáuh
there isn't.../ there aren't any...	没有...	mòh....
these	這些	je-sē
they	他們	tā-mùhn
thief	小偷	síu-tāu
third	第三	daih-sāam

English – Cantonese

English – Cantonese

thirsty: to be thirsty	渴了	hot-líuh	tights	褲襪	foo-maht
thirteen	十三	sahp-sāam	time	時間	sih-gāan
thirty	三十	sāam-sahp	what time is it?	幾點了？	géi-dím-líuh?
this	這個	je-go	timetable	時刻表	sih-hāk-bíu
those	那些	náh-sē	to tip (waiter)	給小費	kāp siu-fai
thousand	一千	yāt-chīn	tip (for service)	小費	siu-fai
three	三	sāam	tobacco	香煙	hēung-yīn
throat	喉嚨	hàuh-lùhng	tobacconist's	香煙店	hēung-yīn-dim
Thursday	星期四	sīng-kèih-sih	today	今天	gām-tīn
ticket (bus, train, etc)	車票	chē-piu	toilet	厠所	chi-so
			tomato	番茄	fāan-kèh
a single ticket	單程票	dāan-chìhng-piu	tomato (tin)	番茄罐頭	fāan-kèh-goon-tàuh
			tomorrow	明天	mìhng-tīn
a return ticket	往返票	wóhng-fáan-piu	tongue	舌頭	siht-tàuh
			tonight	今晚	gām-máahn
student ticket	學生票	hohk-sāang-piu	tooth	牙	ngàh
			toothache	牙痛	ngàh-tung
ticket office	售票處	sauh-piu-chyu	toothbrush	牙刷	ngàh-chaat

English	Chinese	Romanization
toothpaste	牙膏	ngàh-gōu
tourist information	游客資訊	yàuh-haak jí-sun
toy shop	玩具店	wuhn-geuih-dim
toys	玩具	wuhn-geuih
traffic lights	交通燈	gāau-tūng-dāng
train	火車	fó-chē
trainers	運動鞋	wahn-duhng-hàaih
to translate	翻譯	fāan-yihk
to travel	旅行	lúih-hàhng
travel agent's	旅行社	lúih-hàhng-séh
trolley (luggage)	行李推車	hàhng-léih-tūi-chē
trousers	褲子	fu-jí
t-shirt	T恤衫	T-sŭt-sāam
Tuesday	星期二	sing-kèih-yih
to turn off (light, etc)	關	gwāan
to turn on (light, etc)	開	hōi
twelve	十二	sahp-yih
twenty	二十	yih-sahp
two	二	yih
two thousand	兩千	léuhng-chīn
tyre	輪胎	lùhn-tōi
U		
umbrella	雨傘	yúh-saan
underground (metro)	地鉄	deih-tit
underpants	內衣褲	dái-sāam-foo
to understand	明白	mihng-baahk
I don't understand	我不明白	ngóh ngh mihng-baahk

English – Cantonese

English – Cantonese

English	Cantonese	Romanization
do you understand?	你明白嗎?	néih mìhng-baahk mā?
United Kingdom	英國	yìng-gwok
United States	美國	méih-gwok
university	大學	daaih-hohk
unleaded (petrol)	無鉛汽油	mòh-yùehn-hei-yàu
to unlock	開鎖	hōi-só
up	上	seuhng
urgent	緊急的	gán-gāp-dik
us	我們	ngóh-mùhn
to use	使用	sái-yuhng
V		
vacancy (in hotel)	空房	hūng-fòhng
vacation	度假	douh-gáh
valid	有效的	yáuh-haauh-dīk
valuable	有價值的	yáuh-ga-jihk-dīk
value	價值	ga-jihk
vegan	純素食者	sùhn-so-sihk-jé
vegetables	蔬菜	sō-choi
vegetarian	素食者	so-sihk-jé
video camera	錄像機	luhk-jeuhng-gēi
video cassette/tape	錄像帶	luhk-seung-daai
villa	別墅	biht-seuih
village	鄉村	hēung-chyūn
vinegar	醋	cho
virus	病毒	behng-duhk
visa	簽証	chim-jihng
to visit	探訪	taam-fóng

English		Cantonese
voice	聲音	sìng-yàm
to vomit	嘔吐	áu-tou
W		
to wait (for)	等	dáng
waiter/	服務員	fuhk-moh-
waitress		yuehn
walk	步行	boh-hàhng
wall	牆	chèuhng
wallet	錢包	chìhn-bāau
to want	想	séung
I want...	我想…	ngóh séung...
we want...	我們想…	ngóh-mùhn
		séung...
warm	溫暖的	wàn-nuéhn-
		dìk
to wash	洗	sái
washing machine	洗衣機	sái-yì-gēi

English		Cantonese
wasp sting	黃蜂叮刺	wòhng-fūng
		dīng-chì
watch	手錶	sáu-bīu
water	水	séui
boiled water	滾水	gwán-séui
cold water	冷水	láahng-séui
drinking water	飲用水	yám-yuhng-séui
hot water	熱水	yiht-séui
mineral water	礦泉水	kwong-
		chùehn-séui
watermelon	西瓜	sāi-gwā
way in	入口	yahp-háu
way out	出口	chùt-háu
we	我們	ngóh-mùhn
to wear	穿	chūen
weather	天氣	tìn-hei
weather forecast	天氣預報	tìn-hei yuh-
		bo
wedding	婚禮	fàn-láih

English - Cantonese

Wednesday	星期三	sīng-keih-sāam	
week	星期	sīng-keih	
weekend	週末	jāu-muht	
weekly	每週	múih-jāu	
welcome	歡迎	fūn-yìhng	
you're welcome!	不用客氣!	ngh-sái haak-hei!	
west	西方	sāi-fōng	
what	甚麼	sahm-mō	
what is it?	那是甚麼?	sahm-mō?	
wheel	車輪	chē-lùhn	
when	甚麼時候	sahm-mō sih-hauh	
when does it open?	郵局甚麼時間開門?	yàu-guhk sahm-mō sih-gāan hōi-mùhn?	
where	哪裏	náh-léih	
where are you from?	你是哪裏人?	néih-sih náh-léih-yàhn?	
where is...? / Where are ...?	...在哪裏?	...joih náh-léih?	
which	哪一個	náh-yāt-go	
whisky	威士忌酒	wāi-sih-géi-jáu	
white	白色的	baahk-sīk-dīk	
white wine	白葡萄酒	baahk pàh-tòh-jáu	
who	誰	sèuih	
whose: whose is it?	那是誰的?	náh sih seuih-dīk?	
why	為甚麼	waih-sahm-mō	
wife	妻子	chāi-jí	
to win	贏	yèhng	
wind	風	fūng	
window	窗戶	chēung-wuh	

windscreen	擋風玻璃	dóng-fùng-bōh-léih	without ice	不加冰	ngh-gā-bīng
windscreen washer	擋風玻璃清洗器	dóng-fùng-bōh-léih-chīng-sái-hei	without milk	不加奶	ngh-gā-náaih
windscreen wiper	擋風玻璃刮水器	dóng-fùng-bōh-léih-gwaat-séui-hei	without sugar	不加糖	ngh-gā-tòhng
wine	葡萄酒	pòh-tòh-jáu	wok	炒菜鍋	cháau-choi-wòh
red wine	紅葡萄酒	hùhng pòh-tòh-jáu	woman	女仕	nèuih-sih
white wine	白葡萄酒	baahk- pòh-tòh-jáu	work	工作	gūng-jok
winter	冬天	dūng-tìn	world	世界	sai-gaai
with	和/加	wòh/gā	write: please write it down	請把它寫下來	chíng-bá-tā-sé-hah-lòih
with ice	加冰	gā-bīng	wrong	錯誤說的	cho-ngh-dīk
with milk	加奶	gā-náaih			
with sugar	加糖	gā-tòhng	**X**		
without	不加	ngh-gā	x-ray	X光	x-gwōng
			to x-ray	照X光	jiu-x-gwōng
			Y		
			year	年	nìhn
			this year	今年	gām-nìhn

English – Cantonese

English – Cantonese

next year	明年	mihng-nìhn
last year	去年	heui-nìhn
yellow	黃色的	wòhng-sìk-dìk
yes	是	sih
yes, please	好，謝謝	hó, jeh-jeh
yesterday	昨天	johk-tìn
yet: not yet	還沒有	wàahn-muht-yóuh
yoghurt	酸奶	syùn-náaih
you	你/你們	néih/néih-mùhn
and you?	你呢?	néih-nē?
young	年輕的	nìhn-hìng-dìk
your	你的/你們的	néih-dìk/néih-mùhn-dìk

Z

zero	零	lìhng
zone	區域	kēui-wìhk
zoo	動物園	duhng-maht-yùehn

English – Cantonese

Further titles in Collins' phrasebook range
Collins Gem phrasebook

Also available as **phrasebook CD Pack**
Other titles in the series:

Arabic	Greek	Polish
Cantonese	Italian	Portuguese
Croatian	Japanese	Russian
Czech	Korean	Spanish
Dutch	Latin American	Thai
French	Spanish	Turkish
German	Mandarin	Vietnamese

Collins phrasebook & Dictionary

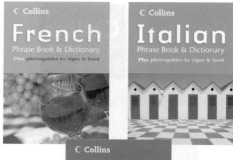

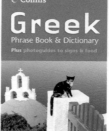

Also available as **phrasebook CD Pack**
Other titles in the series:
German Japanese Portuguese Spanish